CHRIST CHURCH
COLLEGE
CANTERBURY

# The Funny Family

## Songs, Rhymes and Games for Children

## Alison McMorland

### Illustrations by Kevin Maddison

Ward Lock Educational

ISBN 0 7062 3719 6

First published 1978

Text set in Baskerville by Computacomp (UK) Limited
Music set by Halstan & Company Limited
Printed by Hollen Street Press Limited at Slough, Berkshire
for Ward Lock Educational
116 Baker Street, London WIM 2BB
A member of the Pentos Group
Made in Great Britain

# Acknowledgments

I should like to thank all the children and adults who have been my source of material and in particular the following for their contributions:

Mrs Jennie Wheatley of York for nos. 1, 2, 4, 6, 13, 16, 24, 25, 27, 66, 79
Mrs Coverdale of Sherrif Hutton, Yorkshire for no. 10
Mrs Freda Palmer of Witney, Oxfordshire for nos. 23, 67, 77, 80
Mrs Peggy Hillary, originally from Dublin, for no. 70
Mr Bob Cann of South Tawton, Devon for no. 78
Mr Thornton of the valley of Lothersdale, Yorkshire for nos. 29, 69, 71, 74
Mr Mawson also from the valley of Lothersdale, Yorkshire for nos. 72 and 74
'Bobby Shaftoe' from *Whittaker North Countrie Folk Songs* reprinted by permission of Faber Music Limited (for J. Curwen & Sons, Limited).
No. 7 was taken from *Nursery Rhymes and Country Songs* by M. Mason, Metzler, London, 1877.

I should also like to thank Peter Bullock for his patient transcribing of the melodies, piano arrangements and guitar chords.

A selection of the songs and games in this book can be heard on a long-playing record by Alison McMorland entitled *The Funny Family* (Big Ben BBX 504 stereo, cassette BBX MC 504). This is the first in a series of records devoted to songs and games for children. Details of future releases can be obtained from: Big Ben, Tangent Records Limited, 176a Holland Road, London W14 8AH.

# Contents

## Singing Games

Introduction

## Folk Songs

Introduction

Index of first lines

# Guitar chords used in the book

In some cases the guitar chords do not appear to correspond with the key of the piece. This is because they have been simplified by use of a capo. The following chords are used:

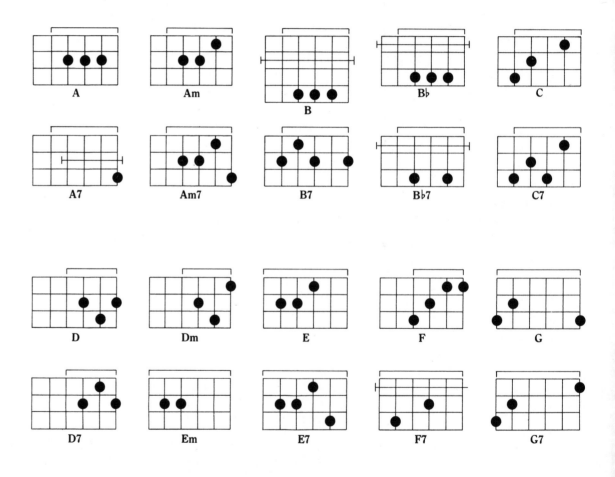

# Foreword

This is a personal collection of songs and games which I have found to be popular with children up to the age of eleven, and has come about through my experience as a folk singer and collector of traditional material. My main source for the collection has been people both little and big – from children showing me their favourite singing games which they play in the street and playground, to grandparents and traditional singers remembering the songs and games of their childhood. The collection ranges from nursery rhymes and action songs to singing games and folk songs, and is a source book of singing material for use with children.

Although this collection and the accompanying notes are intended for the benefit of the child, I hope that the reader, whether parent or teacher, will enjoy using these songs and take pleasure in singing them. They haven't been written by professional musicians for trained singers; rather they have evolved from ordinary people, as an extension of themselves and their lives, through a natural enjoyment of singing.

In singing these songs, is an accompaniment necessary? I don't think so, even though I have included guitar chords for all the songs and simple piano arrangements for the most suitable. A piano creates a physical barrier between teacher and children, and unless playing the piano or guitar is second nature and unobtrusive as an accompaniment only, sing unaccompanied. Spontaneity is the essential essence of this material which could be restricted by a faltering piano, or if the song becomes the vehicle for instrumental development providing a rigid accompaniment. After all, this is how these songs and games were originally sung, for embodied in the words and music are the values, attitudes and humour of our culture. They are our common heritage, to be sung, enjoyed and valued as such.

Alison McMorland

# Nursery Rhymes and Action Songs

Our rhymes of the nursery appear in many book collections handsomely illustrated, but, in the case of the songs, wrongly divorced from their traditional tunes. In many cases the compilers of such books have been unaware of these tunes, their sources having been older printed collections of nursery rhymes. And so we are presented with the predicament of the perpetuation of the printed word which relies on the memory to supply the tune, if known. I hope this small selection supplies some of the lesser-known ones. In many cases the melodies are old, coming from our common store of folk airs, and have become vehicles to carry sets of words adapted through the use of many generations. The Opies (1951) have already drawn attention to the fact that many of the songs which have survived in the nursery are in fact 'unrelated snatches of worldly songs', which the adult will use or adapt when the children have to be amused. This can be seen when it is realized that a relation to the knee-riding song 'O Kafoozalum' is still commonly sung in the Navy.

Nursery rhymes are the child's first introduction to the language of poetry and rhythm of music, through which he becomes aware of a world of fantasy which exists beyond himself. Through the pattern of sounds, inflection and tone of voice, the child learns to recognize varying emotions, while at the same time learning certain fundamental communicative and social skills. However, an equally important aspect is the flow of feeling experienced as the child is played with, or sung to, on his parent's or grandparent's knee. Often a song or game is used from the adult's own childhood, which, along with the physical warmth and closeness, colours the impression made on the child. In years to come a link in a chain will be added if this same child re-enacts a similar situation.

It is essential to know these songs by heart, and to make them meaningful to the young child, where possible, by using his name in the song, or patting his feet or hands, rocking or jogging the child. Rhymes like 'O dearie me' and 'Sing, sing, what shall I sing?' are likely to pop up in the course of the day, as something happens to make you say, 'Oh dearie me'. Don't keep the singing of songs and saying of rhymes to special times; let them flow naturally into the pattern of the day – as you are working, or need to distract the child, in dressing, feeding or whatever. Although very young children will particularly enjoy this section, many of the other songs, and especially the singing games, will also give them great pleasure.

**Reference**
OPIE, I. and P. (1951) *The Oxford Dictionary of Nursery Rhymes* Oxford University Press

# 1 Sing, sing, what shall I sing?

Sing, sing, what shall I sing? The
cat's run a – way with the pud – ding – bag string.

Sing, sing, what shall I sing?
The cat's run away with the pudding-bag string!
Do, do, what shall I do?
The dog has bitten it right in two!

# 2   Round and round the mulberry bush

Round and round the mulberry bush,
  The monkey chased the weasel;
The cobbler kissed the farmer's wife,
  Pop! goes the weasel.

Every night when I go out,
  The monkey's on the table;
Take a stick and knock him off,
  Pop! goes the weasel.

Round and round the mul-ber-ry bush, The mon-key chased the wea-sel; The cob-bler kissed the farm-er's wife, Pop! goes the wea-sel. Ev-ery night when I go out, The mon-key's on the ta-ble; Take a stick and knock him off, Pop! goes the wea-sel.

# 3 There was an old woman tossed up in a blanket

There was an old woman tossed up in a blanket,
Seventeen times as high as the moon;
Where she was going I couldn't but ask,
For in her hand she carried a broom.
'Old woman, old woman, old woman,' says I,
'Whither, O whither, O whither so high?'
'To brush the cobwebs from the sky.'
'O may I go with you?'
'Aye, by-and-by.'

# 4 I had a little pony

I had a little pony, his name was Dapple Grey;
I lent him to a lady to ride a mile away.
She whipped him and she lashed him,
And drove him through the mire;
I wouldn't lend my pony now, for all that lady's
hire.

    So trot, trot, trot my pony,
    So trot, trot, trot away,
    So trot, trot, trot my pony,
    So trot, trot, trot away.

# 5 I wish I had some money

*Capo: 3rd fret*

I wish I had some money, a stable and some hay,
I'd buy a Shetland pony, and ride him every day.
With neither spur nor whip,
I'd give him just a click, click, click (*click tongue*).
  Come trot, trot, trot my pony,
  Come trot, trot, trot I say,
  Come trot, trot, trot my pony,
  Come trot, trot, trot away.

# 6  I had a little cock

I had a little cock and the cock pleased me,
I fed my cock down under the tree,
    And the cock went cockery crow,
Join in every neighbour's cock
And my one well done too.

I had a little hen and the hen pleased me,
I fed my hen down under the tree,
    And the hen went chuck chuck,
    The cock went cockery crow,
Join in every neighbour's cock
And my one well done too.

I had a little duck … (quack, quack)

I had a little goose … (sss, sss)

I had a little chick … (cheep, cheep)

*Add more animals*

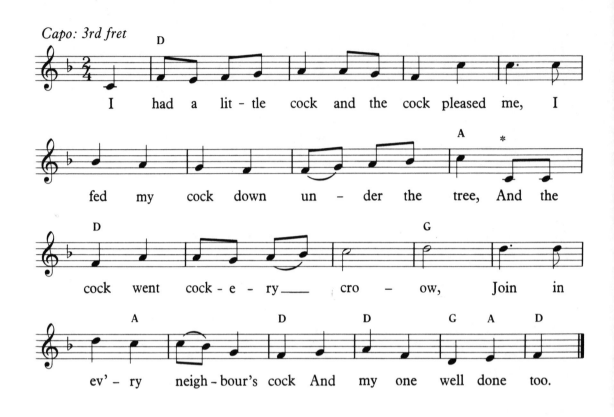

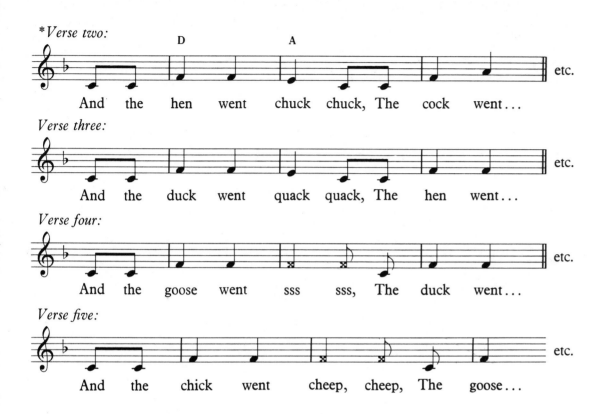

And     the     hen     went     chuck     chuck,     The     cock     went...     etc.

*Verse three:*

And     the     duck     went     quack     quack,     The     hen     went...     etc.

*Verse four:*

And     the     goose     went     sss     sss,     The     duck     went...     etc.

*Verse five:*

And     the     chick     went     cheep,     cheep,     The     goose...     etc.

# 7 Dickery, dickery, dock

Dickery, dickery, dock, dock, dock,
The mouse ran up the clock, clock, clock.
The clock struck one, and down the mouse ran;
So dickery, dickery, dock, dock, dock.

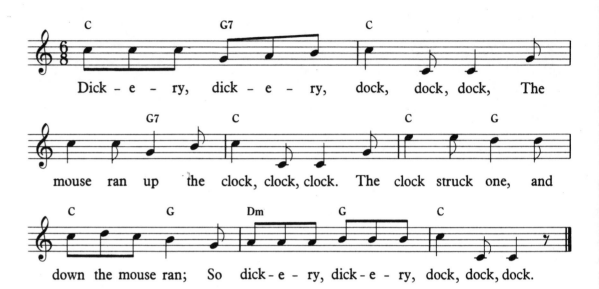

# 8 Up in the north

*Capo: 3rd fret*

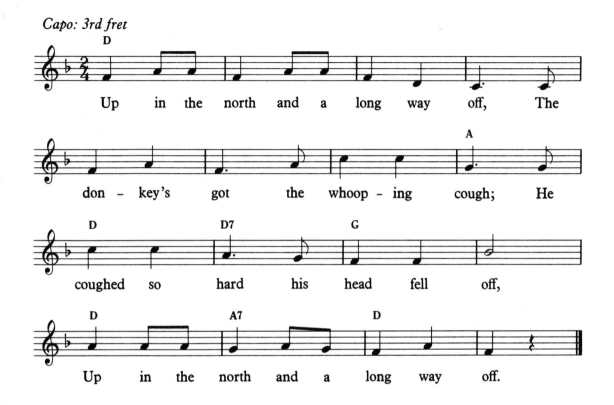

Up in the north and a long way off, The
don – key's got the whoop – ing cough; He
coughed so hard his head fell off,
Up in the north and a long way off.

Up in the north and a long way off,
The donkey's got the whooping cough;
He coughed so hard his head fell off,
Up in the north and a long way off.

# 9   If I had a donkey

If I had a donkey and he wouldn't go,
Do you think I would whip him? Oh no, no.
I'd put him in the barn and give him some corn,
The best little donkey that ever was born.

If I had another and he wouldn't go,
Do you think I would whip him? Oh no, no.
I'd put him in the barn and give him some straw,
And my two little donkeys would say hee-haw.

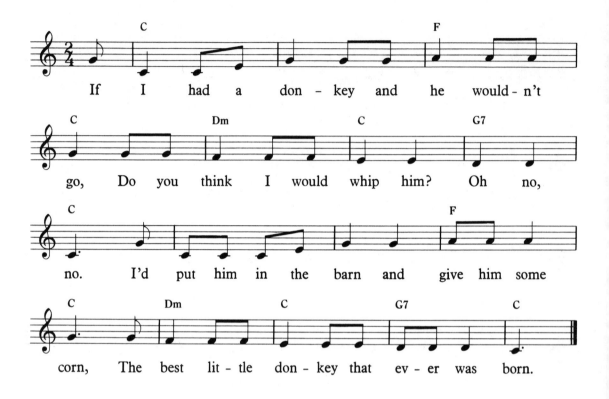

*Your child will enjoy riding on your knee to these next tunes.*

# 10 O Kafoozalum

O_____ Ka - foo - za - lum, Ka - foo - za - lum,

O_____ Ka - foo - za - lum, rid - ing on me don - key.

I'm a sol - dier you can see, Just in time for a

cup of tea. Now I'm out up - on a spree, Rid - ing on me

don - key. O_____ Ka - foo - za - lum, Ka - foo - za - lum,

O_____ Ka - foo - za - lum, be - cause I got off me don - key.

O Kafoozalum, Kafoozalum,
O Kafoozalum, riding on me donkey.
I'm a soldier you can see,
Just in time for a cup of tea.
Now I'm out upon a spree,
Riding on me donkey.
O Kafoozalum, Kafoozalum,
O Kafoozalum, because I got off me donkey.

# 11  Mrs Sippy-o

O Mrs Sippy-o,
Had a little baby-o,
Dresses it in calico,
Riding on a donkey.

O Mrs Eppelwhite
Are you coming out tonight?
You look such a bonny sight,
Riding on a donkey.

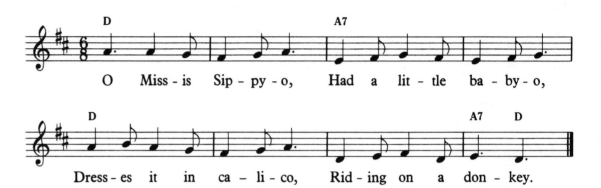

# 12 Hokey pokey

*Capo: 1st fret*

Ho-key, po-key, pen-ny a lump, That's the stuff to make you jump.

If you jump you're sure to fall, Ho-key, po-key, that's it all.

Hokey, pokey, penny a lump,
That's the stuff to make you jump.
If you jump you're sure to fall,
  Hokey, pokey, that's it all.

On the word 'all', separate your knees and
let the child fall through your lap.

# 13 Johnny was a soldier

Johnny was a soldier,
Johnny was a soldier,
Johnny was a soldier,
   I-O! I-O! I-O!

And he went a-marching,
He went a-marching,
He went a-marching,
   I-O! I-O! I-O!

We'll all be little soldiers,
We'll all be little soldiers,
We'll all be little soldiers,
   I-O! I-O! I-O!

So we'll go a-marching,
We'll go a-marching,
We'll go a-marching,
   I-O! I-O! I-O!

John – ny was a sol – dier, John – ny was a sol – dier,
John – ny was a sol – dier, I – O! I – O! I – O!

# 14 There was an old woman lived under the stairs

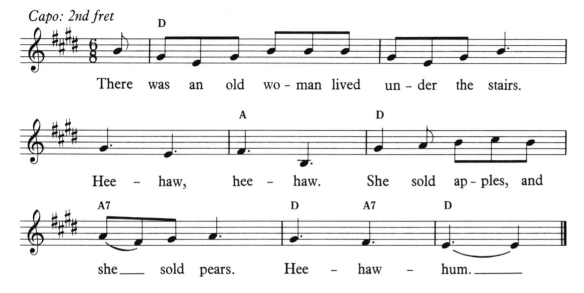

There was an old woman lived under the stairs.
    Hee-haw, hee-haw.
She sold apples, and she sold pears.
    Hee-haw-hum.

All her bright money she laid on the shelf.
    Hee-haw, hee-haw.
If you want any more you can sing it yourself.
    Hee-haw-hum.

# 15 It's raining, it's pouring

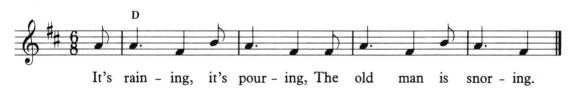

It's raining, it's pouring,
    The old man is snoring.
He went to bed to mend his head,
    And couldn't get up in the morning.
The doctor came and pulled the chain,
    And up came the puffa-train.

# 16  A little cock sparrow

A little cock sparrow sat up in a tree,
And he chirruped, and chirruped, so merry was he.
Till a little boy came with his wee bow and arrow,
And said I will shoot that little cock sparrow.

His head it will make a nice little stew,
And his body will make me a nice pie too.
Oh, no, said the sparrow, that never will do,
So he spread out his wings and away he flew.

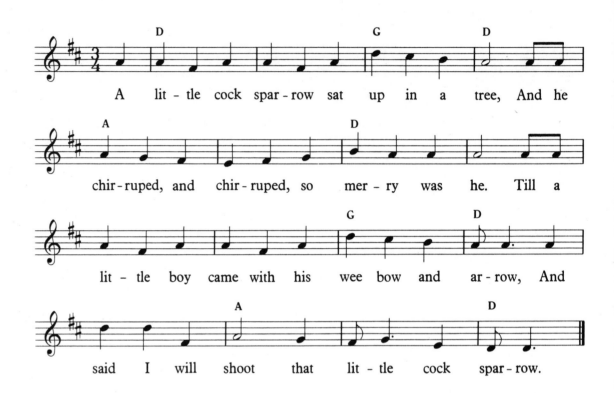

# 17 Old King Coul

*Capo: 3rd fret*

Old King Coul was a merry old soul,
And a merry old soul was he.
He called for his pipe and he called for his bowl
And he called for his fiddlers three.
Fiddle, diddle, fiddle, diddle, said the fiddlers three.
   Oh, there's no a lass in all Scotland,
   Like our sweet Marjorie.

Old King Coul was a merry old soul,
And a merry old soul was he.
He called for his pipe and he called for his bowl
And he called for his drummers three.
Rub-a-dub-a, rub-a-dub-a, went the drummers
   three,
Fiddle, diddle, fiddle, diddle, said the fiddlers three.
   Oh, there's no a lass in all Scotland,
   Like our sweet Marjorie.

*... and so on, adding a new instrument.*

# 18 When good King Arthur ruled this land

When good King Arthur ruled this land,
   He was a goodly king;
He stole three pecks of barley-meal
   To make a bag-pudding.

A bag-pudding the Queen she made,
   And stuffed it full of plums;
And in it put great lumps of fat,
   As big as both my thumbs.

The king and queen sat down to dine,
   And all the court beside;
And what they could not eat that night,
   The queen next morning fried.

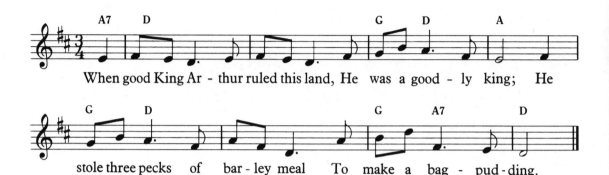

When good King Ar - thur ruled this land, He was a good - ly king; He stole three pecks of bar - ley meal To make a bag - pud - ding.

As I was walking down Iccy-piccy lane,
I met some Iccy-piccy people.

# 19 Mrs White had a fright

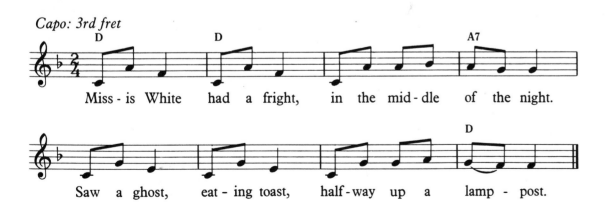

*Capo: 3rd fret*

Miss - is White had a fright, in the mid - dle of the night.

Saw a ghost, eat - ing toast, half - way up a lamp - post.

Mrs White had a fright, in the middle of the night.
Saw a ghost, eating toast, half-way up a lamp-post.

Mrs Black got the sack, said she wasn't coming back.
Mrs Green saw the Queen, on the television screen.

Mrs Brown went to town, with her knickers
    hanging down.
Mrs Red went to bed, and in the morning she was
    dead.

*Make up some more rhymes to go with Mrs Blue, Pink, etc.*

# 20  Sam, Sam, the mucky old man

Sam, Sam, the mucky old man,
Washed his face in the frying pan.
Combed his hair with a donkey's tail,
And scratched his belly with his big toe-nail.

# 21 O dearie me

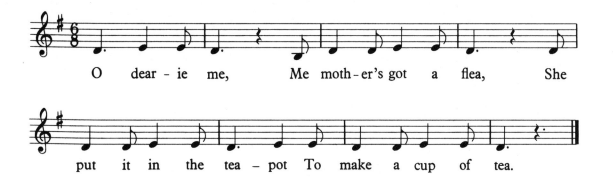

O dearie me,
Me mother's got a flea,
She put it in the teapot
   To make a cup of tea.
The flea jumped out,
Me mother did shout,
In came me brother
   With his shirt hanging out.

# 22 O can you wash your father's shirt?

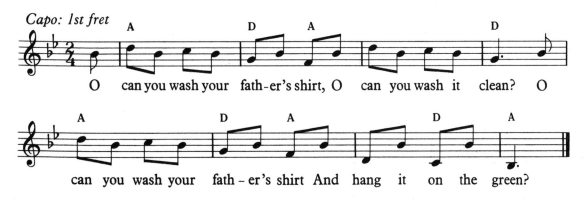

O can you wash your father's shirt,
O can you wash it clean?
O can you wash your father's shirt
   And hang it on the green?
O I can wash my father's shirt,
O I can wash it clean.
O I can wash my father's shirt
   And hang it on the green.

# 23 A little bird built a warm nest in a tree

A little bird built a warm nest in a tree,
And laid some blue eggs in it, one, two and three.
And very much pleased and delighted was she,
And very much pleased and delighted was she.

She spread her soft wings over them all the day long,
To warm and to guide them her love was so strong.
And her mate sat beside her and sang her a song,
And her mate sat beside her and sang her a song.

One day the poor birds all crying for food,
So out flew the mother, away from her brood.
Then up came some boys who were wicked and rude,
Then up came some boys who were wicked and rude.

They tore the warm nest away from the tree,
The little ones cried but they could not get free.
And so they all died away, one, two and three,
And so they all died away, one, two and three.

And when back again the poor mother did fly,
O then she set up a most pitiful cry.
She mourned a long time, then she lay down and died,
She mourned a long time, then she lay down and died.

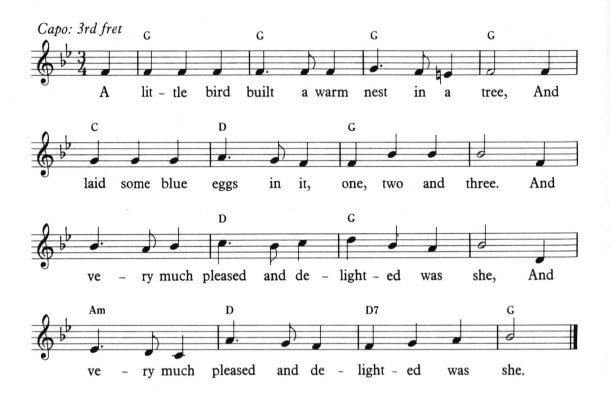

# 24 Bee-o, bee-o

Bee – o, bee – o, bon – ny, bon – ny, bee – o;

Bee – o, bee – o, bon – ny babe o' mine.__ I

love my lit – tle gir – lie, Your hair is nice and cur – ly. I

love you, I love you, I love you 'cos you're mine. __

Bee – o, bee – o, bon – ny, bon – ny, bee – o;

Bee – o, bee – o, I love you 'cos you're mine. __

Bee-o, bee-o, bonny, bonny, bee-o;
Bee-o, bee-o, bonny babe o' mine.

I love my little girlie,
Your hair is nice and curly.
I love you, I love you,
I love you 'cos you're mine.
    Bee-o, bee-o, bonny, bonny, bee-o;
    Bee-o, bee-o, I love you 'cos you're mine.

I love my little boy,
Oh you're daddy's pride and joy,
I love you, I love you,
I love you 'cos you're mine.
    Bee-o, bee-o, bonny, bonny, bee-o;
    Bee-o, bee-o, I love you 'cos you're mine.

Good night, sleep tight,
Don't let the bugs bite,
    If they bite
    SQUEEZE them tight!
Good night.

# 25 Cuckoo! cherry tree

Cu – ckoo! cher-ry tree, Catch the ball, Throw to me.

Cuckoo! cherry tree,
Catch the ball,
Throw to me.

Attract the child's attention,
throw large ball to child,
child throws it back.

# 26 Two little dicky birds

Two little dicky birds, sitting on a wall;
One named Peter, one named Paul.
Fly away, Peter! Fly away, Paul!
Come back, Peter! Come back, Paul!

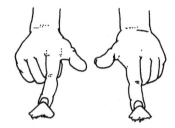

Stick a small piece of paper on the nail of your index fingers (the gummed edge of an envelope is good for this) and tuck your other fingers into the palm of each hand. Hold up both your fingers, naming one 'Peter' and the other 'Paul'.

At 'Fly away' toss each appropriate hand over your shoulder out of sight, and at 'Come back' bring it back with the middle finger in place of the index finger. Where have 'Peter' and 'Paul' gone to?

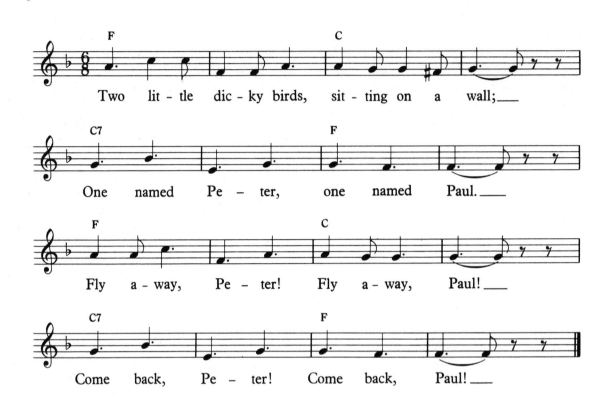

Two lit-tle dic-ky birds, sit-ting on a wall;___

One named Pe-ter, one named Paul.___

Fly a-way, Pe-ter! Fly a-way, Paul!___

Come back, Pe-ter! Come back, Paul!___

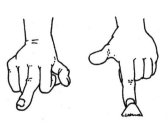

# 27 Thumbkin

*Capo: 3rd fret*

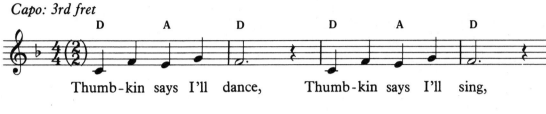

Thumb-kin says I'll dance,    Thumb-kin says I'll sing,

Danc-ing, sing-ing, mer-ry lit-tle men, Thumb-kin says I'll dance and sing.

Thumbkin says I'll dance,
Thumbkin says I'll sing,
Dancing, singing, merry little men,
Thumbkin says I'll dance and sing.

Pointer says I'll dance,
Pointer says I'll sing,
Dancing, singing, merry little men,
Pointer says I'll dance and sing.

Middleman says I'll dance,
Middleman says I'll sing ...

Ringman says I'll dance,
Ringman says I'll sing ...

Littleman says I'll dance,
Littleman says I'll sing ...

Show first thumb, then
second thumb.
Wag thumbs towards each other.

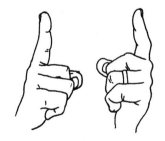

Show first pointing finger, then
second pointing finger.
Wag pointing fingers towards each other

Show first middle finger, then
second middle finger ...

Show first ring finger, then
second ring finger ...

Show first little finger, then
second little finger ...

# 28  Here's the church

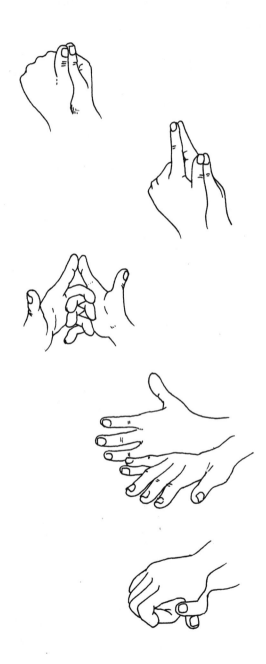

Interlock your fingers and enclose them in the cupped palms of your hands, your knuckles suggesting the roof of a church and keeping your thumbs upright and close together.

Raise both index fingers and hold them tip to tip.

Your thumbs are the 'doors' which when opened show a congregation of wagging fingers.

Cross your wrists making your hands back to back.
Link the two little fingers, then the ring, middle and pointing fingers until all are interlaced.
Drop your hands forward and bring your palms together; wrap the left thumb round the right thumb, which should be sticking up like a preacher in a pulpit. Now the tricky part – pull your hands through and bring them to rest under your chin and wag the parson at the congregation as he delivers his prayer.

Here's the church

And here's the steeple,

Open the door
And here's the people.

Here's the parson
Climbing the stairs,

And here he is
Saying his prayers.

Dearly beloved bretheren,
    Isn't it a sin,
When we peel potatoes
    We throw away the skin.
The skin feeds the pigs,
    And the pigs feed you.
Dearly beloved bretheren,
    Now isn't this true?

There is also a tune to 'Dearly beloved
bretheren' if you want to make him into a
singing parson.

# 29 Dearly beloved bretheren

Dearly beloved bretheren,
  Isn't it a sin,
When we peel potatoes
  We throw away the skin.
The skin feeds the pigs,
  And the pigs feed you.
Dearly beloved bretheren,
  Now isn't this true?

# 30 Sandy-o

Sandy-o, Sandy-o,
 Diddle-aye, diddle-aye, diddle-aye-o.
There was a man, a man indeed,
 Sowed his garden full of seeds.
When the seeds began to grow,
 Like a garden full of snow,
When the snow began to melt,
 Like a ship without a belt,
When the ship began to sail,
 Like a bird without a tail,
When the bird began to fly,
 Time for me to say goodbye.
  Pop goes one, Pop goes two,
  Pop my hand right over you!

With the child on your knee, teach him to
clap to this song. It may be simpler for you
to hold your hands up with the palms facing
him, while he just does the clapping, but
here is the clapping routine for two players.

Clap your own hands together – clap each
other's right hand.
Clap your own hands together – clap each
other's left hand.
Repeat pattern.

On the last line, cover partner's eyes with
palm of right hand.

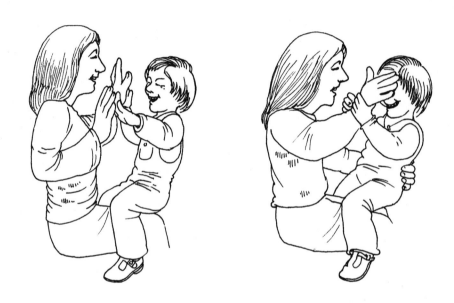

*And here are two more songs to clap to, using the same tune.*

# 31 My mother says I must go

My mother says I must go
  With my daddy's dinner-o.
Baked tatters, a bit of steak,
  A wee bit of ham and a currant cake.
I came to a river and I couldn't get across,
  I paid ten shillings for an old lame hoss.
I jumped on his back,
  His bones gave a crack;
We all played the fiddle
  Till the boat came back.

# 32 There was a man, he was mad

There was a man, he was mad,
  He jumped into a paper bag.
The paper bag was too narrow,
  He jumped into a wheelbarrow.
The wheelbarrow ran away,
  Bumped into a cart of hay.
The cart of hay caught on fire,
  He jumped into a cow's byre.
The cow's byre was too nasty,
  He jumped into an apple pasty.
The apple pasty fell off the plate,
  He jumped right into Harrogate.
Harrogate was full of stones
  And they broke the mad man's bones.

# 33 A sailor went to sea

A sailor went to sea, sea, sea,
To see what he could see, see, see,
But all that he could see, see, see,
Was the bottom of the deep blue sea, sea, sea.

A sailor went to chop, chop, chop,
To see what he could chop, chop, chop,
But all that he could chop, chop, chop,
Was the bottom of the deep blue chop, chop, chop.

A sailor went to knee, knee, knee,
To see what he could knee, knee, knee …

A sailor went to toe, toe, toe,
To see what he could toe, toe, toe …

A sailor went to heel, heel, heel,
To see what he could heel, heel, heel …

A sailor went to sea, chop, knee, toe, heel,
To see what he could see, chop, knee, toe, heel,
But all that he could see, chop, knee, toe, heel,
Was the bottom of the deep blue sea, chop, knee,
    toe, heel.

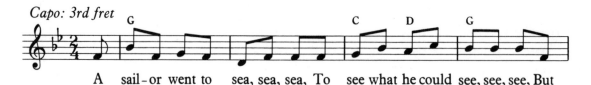

A sail-or went to sea, sea, sea, To see what he could see, see, see, But

all that he could see, see, see, Was the bottom of the deep blue sea, sea, sea.

On the words *sea, sea, sea*, salute forehead
with right hand in rhythm with words –
three times on each line of verse.

On *chop, chop, chop* in second verse, chop
crook of right arm.

Touch knee, toe, heel as appropriate in
following verses.

In the last verse, touch forehead, arm, knee,
toe, heel – four times over.

# 34 When I was one

When I was one, I ate a bun, The day I went to sea. _____ I jumped a-board a pir - ate ship And the cap - tain said to me, 'I'm go - ing this way, that way, for-wards and back - wards O - ver the I – rish Sea. _____ A bot-tle of rum to fill my tum, That's the life for me.' _____

On the chorus line 'I'm going this way, that way' shade your eyes with your hand and look left and right.

Push arm forwards and pull backwards to next line, and then make wavy motions with hand as if going over the sea.

Pretend to drink from a bottle, and rub 'tum' during the last two lines of the chorus.

When I was one, I ate a bun,
The day I went to sea.
    I jumped aboard a pirate ship
    And the captain said to me,
    'I'm going this way, that way,
    Forwards and backwards
    Over the Irish Sea.
    A bottle of rum to fill my tum,
    That's the life for me.'

When I was two, I buckled my shoe,
The day I went to sea.
    I jumped aboard a pirate ship
    And the captain said to me,
    'I'm going this way, that way,
    Forwards and backwards
    Over the Irish Sea.
    A bottle of rum to fill my tum,
    That's the life for me.'

When I was three, I grazed my knee
The day I went to sea …

When I was four, I knocked at the door,
The day I went to sea …

When I was five, I learned to dive,
The day I went to sea …

When I was six (seven, eight, nine, ten) …

*Make up your own verses.*

# 35 Old Davey Jones

Old Davey Jones had one little sailor,
Old Davey Jones had one little sailor,
Old Davey Jones had one little sailor,
   One little sailor boy.

He had one, he had two, he had three little sailors,
Four, he had five, he had six little sailors,
Seven, he had eight, he had nine little sailors,
   Ten little sailor boys.

Old Davey Jones had ten little sailors ...

He had ten, he had nine, he had eight little sailors,
Seven little, six little, five little sailors,
Four little, three little, two little sailors,
   One little sailor boy.

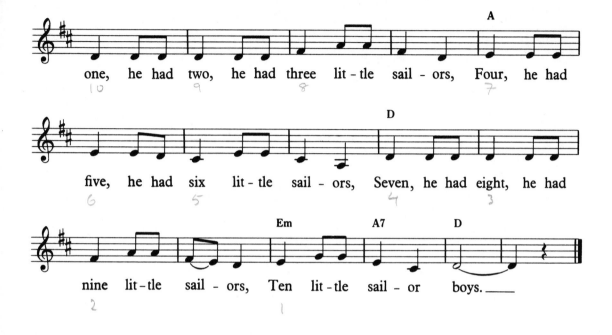

one, he had two, he had three lit – tle sail – ors, Four, he had

five, he had six lit – tle sail – ors, Seven, he had eight, he had

nine lit – tle sail – ors, Ten lit – tle sail – or boys. _____

Tuck the fingers into the palms of your hands, which are turned towards you. Raise one thumb and waggle it for the first verse.

Raise the first finger at two, and the other fingers as they are counted to make ten little sailor boys.

The order of counting can be reversed, tucking the fingers back into the palms again as you count.

# 36 Father William

Father William had seven sons,
Seven sons had Father William,
And they ate a little, and they drank a little,
And they all had lots of fun.
    Right hand.

Father William had seven sons,
Seven sons had Father William,
And they ate a little, and they drank a little,
And they all had lots of fun.
    Right hand, left hand.

Father William had seven sons,
Seven sons had Father William,
And they ate a little, and they drank a little,
And they all had lots of fun.
    Right hand, left hand,
    Right foot.

Father William had seven sons,
Seven sons had Father William,
And they ate a little, and they drank a little,
And they all had lots of fun.
    Right hand, left hand,
    Right foot, left foot.

Father William had seven sons,
Seven sons had Father William,
And they ate a little, and they drank a little,
And they all had lots of fun.
    Right hand, left hand,
    Right foot, left foot,
    NOD YOUR HEAD!

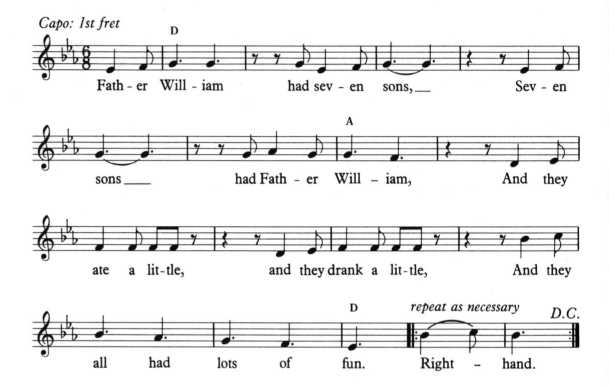

*Capo: 1st fret*

On 'Right hand' at the end of the first verse, pound right hand on right knee and continue doing so through the second verse.

Do the same with the left hand at the end of the second verse and continue with both hands through the third verse.

Stamp right foot up and down at the end of the third verse, while still pounding both hands on knees.

Continue through the fourth verse, adding left foot to the other movements.

At 'NOD YOUR HEAD', do all the actions with hands, feet and head while singing the verse for the last time and then collapse!

# 37 Knicky, knicky, knacky, noo

Put my hand on myself, what have I here?
This is my head knocker, my souvenir.
Head knocker, knicky, knicky, knacky, noo;
  That's what they taught me when I went to
    school.

Put my hand on myself, what have I here?
This is my eye blinker, my souvenir.
Eye blinker, head knocker, knicky, knicky, knacky,
  noo:
  That's what they taught me when I went to
    school.

Put my hand on myself, what have I here?
This is my nose wiper …

This is my tea strainer …

This is my chin chopper …

This is my chest bumper …

This is my bread basket …

This is my thigh bumper …

This is my knee knocker …

This is my toe tapper …

This is my heel wagger …

Starting with the head in the first verse, touch each item in turn as it is sung, gradually progressing down the body – eye, nose, teeth, chin, chest, 'bread basket' (make enormous stomach), 'thigh bumper' (slap thighs), knock knees, toes and heels.

Add on one item in each verse, and try doing the last verse as fast as possible!

# 38   We're going on a bearhunt

*Chorus:*

*Sing*   We're going on a bearhunt. (*leader*)
       *We're going on a bearhunt.* (*group*)
       We're going to catch a big one.
       *We're going to catch a big one.*

*Say*   I'm not scared.
       *I'm not scared.*
       What a beautiful day.
       *What a beautiful day.*
       Oh! Oh!
       *Oh! Oh!*

*Say*   GRASS!
       *Grass!*
       Long, wavy grass.
       *Long, wavy grass.*

*Sing*   We can't go over it.
       *We can't go over it.*
       We can't go under it.
       *We can't go under it.*

*Say*   We'll have to go THROUGH IT! (*all*)
       Ssh! Ssh! Ssh! Ssh!
       Ssh! Ssh! Ssh! Ssh!

*Chorus:*

*Say*   TREES! (*group repeat*)
       Big, tall trees. (*group repeat*)

*Sing*   We can't go over it …

*Say*   We'll have to go THROUGH IT! (*all*)
       Click! Click! Click! Click!
       Click! Click! Click! Click!

*Chorus:*

*Say*   MUD! (*group repeat*)
       Thick, squelchy mud. (*group repeat*)

*Sing*   We can't go over it …

*Say*   We'll have to go THROUGH IT! (*all*)
       Slurp! Slurp! Slurp! Slurp!
       Slurp! Slurp! Slurp! Slurp!

*Chorus:*

*Say*   A CAVE! (*group repeat*)
       A dark, gloomy cave. (*group repeat*)

*Sing*   We can't go over it …

*Say*   We'll have to go THROUGH IT! (*all*)
       X   X   X   X
       X   X   X   X

*Chorus (first six lines) then:*

*Say*   Oh! Oh!
       *Oh! Oh!*

*Sing*   Two black furry ears.
       *Two black furry ears.*
       One black wet nose.
       *One black wet nose.*
       Two sharp pointed teeth.
       *Two sharp pointed teeth.*

*Say*   It's a Bear!
       *It's a Bear!*
       Quick! Run back (*leader only*)
       Through the cave – X   X   X   X
       Through the mud – Slurp! Slurp! Slurp! Slurp!
       Through the trees – Click! Click! Click! Click!
       Through the grass – Ssh! Ssh! Ssh! Ssh!
       Quick back home and slam the door!

*Capo: 1st fret*

**D**

(leader) We're go — ing on a bear — hunt.

(group) We're go — ing on a bear — hunt.

(leader) We're going to catch a big one.

(group) We're going to catch a big one.

(leader) We can't go ov – er it (group) We can't go ov – er it.

(leader) We can't go un – der it (group) We can't go un – der it.

One person leads the others, who copy everything he does in words and actions.

On 'We can't go over it, we can't go under it', use hand to go 'over' and 'under' an imaginary obstacle, and then put hands together and 'dive' through it.

Rub palms of hands together backwards and forwards in time to the words for the sound of grass.

Click with tongue and pretend to climb trees by piling fists one on top of the other for climbing up and down trees.

Make slurping noises for mud by sucking inwards through mouth with tongue vibrating against cheeks.

Click tongue against roof of mouth for going through the cave.

When running back home, the group do the noises and actions in time to the leader's words, and finally all make a banging noise to slam the door!

Take this as a basis for a bearhunt and make up other obstacles on the journey.

# 39 Punchinello's band

Look who comes here, Punchinello little fellow,
  Look who comes here, Punchinello little man.
What can you play, Punchinello little fellow,
  What can you play, Punchinello little man?

    I can play on a paper and comb, (– – – –,
      – – – –)
    I can play on a paper and comb, (– – – – – –)
    We all play on a paper and comb, (– – – –,
      – – – –)
    We all play on a paper and comb. (– – – – – –)

Look who comes here, Punchinello little fellow,
  Look who comes here, Punchinello little man.
What can you play, Punchinello little fellow,
  What can you play, Punchinello little man?

    I can play on a pair of spoons …

    I can play on a mouth organ …

    I can play on a saucepan lid …

    I can play on a triangle …

    I can play on a tamborine …

This song lends itself to the improvisation of
musical instruments – from everyday
kitchen equipment to school percussion.

One person, or group of children, sings the first verse throughout, and is answered by different individuals or groups playing a selection of percussion.

On the seventh and eighth lines everyone joins in pretending to play along with the particular instrument being named.

When all the percussion have been brought in, everyone plays a complete verse together as Punchinello's band.

# Singing Games

Here is a selection of traditional singing games as played by children of today and yesterday. Singing games have evolved through many generations and from different sources. They reflect attitudes and experiences of life, and in some cases retain traces of mythology and ceremony. Two hundred years ago games played by children past early childhood were identical to those played by adults on village greens in the summer, and so we have reason to believe in their antiquity. A clear example of this link with old customs can be seen at Helston, Cornwall, where the town's brass band, playing the 'Furry Dance' tune, leads the dancers along the narrow streets, in through the front doors of the houses and out of the back doors. They are ceremonially bringing good luck to each house as they make a tour of the village. In an earlier time this was known as 'beating the bounds' and after such occasions marriage contracts were arranged. This ceremony is clearly reflected in 'Round and round the village', a game that is still remembered today.

Through the memories of people who were children at the beginning of the century, we know of a variety of elaborate singing games that are no longer played by today's children. Social and economic factors contribute to the patterns of children's play. At the turn of the century, families were larger; the older child was expected to look after the younger ones, and more was demanded from him in working time and other responsibilities. With the absence of heavy traffic, the street was a playground, and the school playground housed children of a wide age range. The child belonged to a community and would initially watch older children playing games that catered for the group. Later he would find himself being guided through them until the time came for him to take over. He would in fact be experiencing the fundamentals of learning – watching and assimilating, participating and finally realizing. Generally speaking, this way of living has gone, and with it some of the games that thrived through the unbroken oral tradition. Today's child experiences greater independence yet he still needs to learn sociability. Belonging to a community group that allows the individual to play a part and making open decisions within this group, are two valuable characteristics of these singing games.

Many teachers are aware of the lack of old communal games that are played in today's playgrounds, and are rightly concerned about it. What positive action can be taken to keep these games alive, apart from the conventional idea of using them in class? In order to develop and benefit from playing these games, children must be able to identify with them, claim and use them as their own. How can a teacher direct this process without allowing the inevitable attitude by the children of 'them and us' deaden the playing of the game? Remembering the traditional way of assimilating, participating and finally realizing, my own approach to this problem would be to give these games back to the children through other children.

Initially I would use the material over a period of time so that words and music become familiar to all. I would choose a small group of older children who are socially good mixers and teach them the game. After the games are established I would designate these children to 'pass them on', allowing time in the curriculum, and a corner of a room or playground to do so, if necessary. This would put the games back into the same setting as the family situation of old, where the older children cared for the younger ones. It is important to keep the groups to a small, manageable number of children to ensure that all have a turn before the majority tire of the game. It is also important to let the children make their own decisions when choosing partners or new people to replace them in the game.

I believe the part these singing games play is an important thread in the child's development; children are natural inheritors of the oral tradition and these games have passed the test of time as well as the test of fulfilling musical and social needs.

# 40 Sally go round the sun

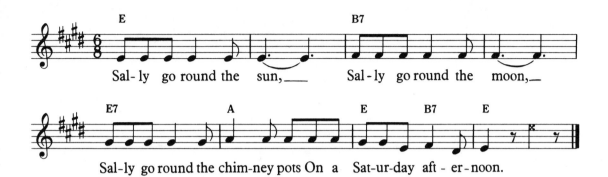

Sal-ly go round the sun,___ Sal-ly go round the moon,__

Sal-ly go round the chim-ney pots On a Sat-ur-day aft - er - noon.

Sally go round the sun,
  Sally go round the moon,
Sally go round the chimney pots
  On a Saturday afternoon.

A small group of six or seven children join hands and whirl around in a circle at quite a fast pace.

On the final line, they kick their legs high in the air and shout. The verse is repeated again with hardly a pause.

You can alternate the direction of the circle, and if the game is going at its full natural rhythm the amount of times the circle can turn is limited.

# 41 Wally, wally, wallflowers

Wally, wally, wallflowers, growing up so high,
We're all young maidens and soon going to die.
Except for (——), she's the only one,
    She can hop, she can sing,
    She can turn a wedding ring.

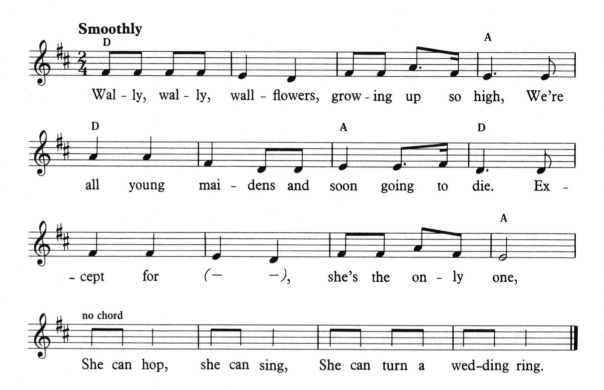

A small group of children hold hands and slowly circle clockwise.

The one who is named turns her back to the circle and continues going around but facing outwards.

This continues until the whole circle is facing outwards.

The procedure can be reversed, until everyone is facing inwards, as at the beginning of the game.

# 42 Rosy had an apple and a pear

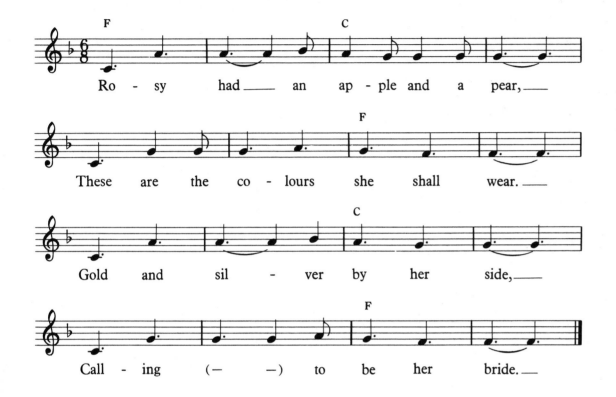

Ro - sy had ___ an ap - ple and a pear, ___

These are the co - lours she shall wear. ___

Gold and sil - ver by her side, ___

Call - ing (— —) to be her bride. ___

Rosy had an apple and a pear,
These are the colours she shall wear.
Gold and silver by her side,
Calling (— —) to be her bride.
   Take her by the lily white hand,
   Take her by the water.
   Give her kisses one, two, three,
   For she is the farmer's daughter.

The children circle around with a boy
standing in the centre.

On the fourth line he names a girl and on
the fifth line the children stand still and
raise their arms to make arches for the
couple to walk under.

He kisses her on the seventh line and rejoins
the ring, leaving the girl to choose a new
sweetheart.

# 43 I've a pigeon in my pocket

I've a pigeon in my pocket
And it won't bite you,
    Won't bite you, won't bite you.
I've a pigeon in my pocket
And it won't bite you,
    But it will bite – YOU !

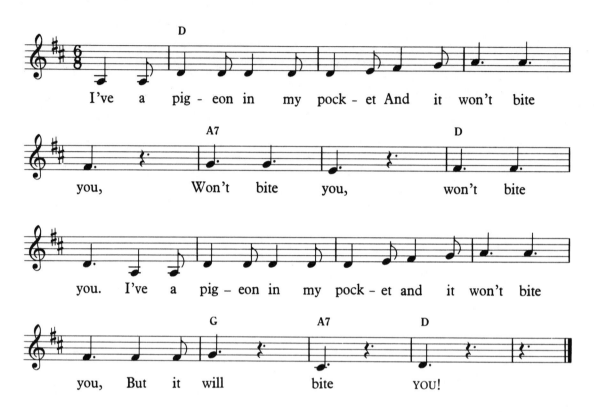

The children sit in a circle and one child skips round the outside carrying a hanky, scarf or piece of paper.

At the final 'you' he drops the hanky behind someone's back, touching that person at the same time, and runs outside the circle. The chosen person with the hanky races around in the opposite direction. Both children are aiming to reach the gap in the circle first. The child who is left starts the game again.

Another version of this game, which is played in the same way, is 'Lucy Locket'.

# 44 Lucy Locket

Lucy Locket lost her pocket,
Kitty Fisher found it.
Not a penny was there in it
But a ribbon round it.

Dree, dree, drop it, drop it,
Dree, dree, drop it, drop it ...
   *(repeat until the hanky has been dropped)*

## 45 Down in the valley

Down in the valley where the green grass grows,
There sits Sally washing her clothes.
She sings, she sings, she sings so sweet,
And calls to (—— ) playing down the street.

(—— ), (—— ), won't you come to tea,
Come next Saturday at half past three,
Ice-cream and jelly you will see,
And there will be lots for you and me.

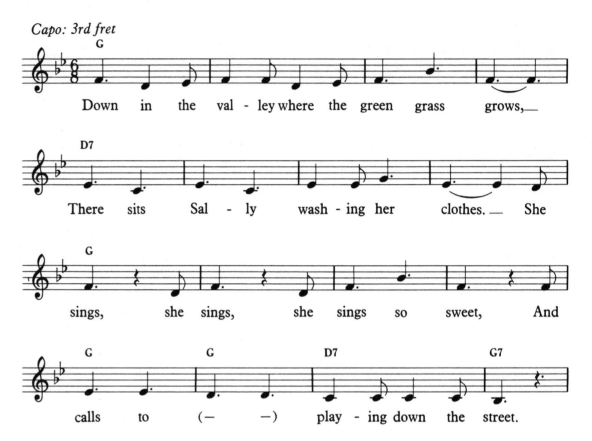

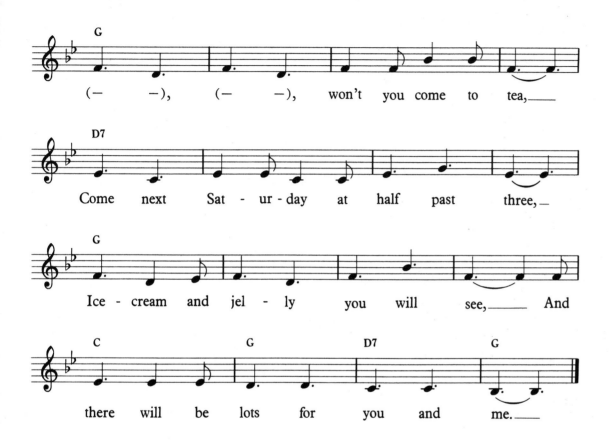

( — — ), ( — — ), won't you come to tea,___

Come next Sat - ur - day at half past three, —

Ice - cream and jel - ly you will see,___ And

there will be lots for you and me.___

The children circle round singing, with one child in the middle who names a child from the circle on the fourth line.

On the fifth line the children sing the new name. The named child joins the one in the centre and, holding hands, they walk around forming a small circle.

The game progresses in this way, and gradually the inner circle grows until the outer circle just walks around unable to hold hands. When the outer circle has diminished to a single person, this child goes into the centre of the now large inner circle, and the game starts again.

# 46 Lazy Katy, will you get up?

Lazy Katy, will you get up,
You get up, you get up?
Lazy Katy, will you get up
This cold and frosty morning?

No, Mother, I won't get up,
Won't get up, won't get up.
No, Mother, I won't get up
This cold and frosty morning.

What if I give you some bread and jam,
Bread and jam, bread and jam?
What if I give you some bread and jam
This cold and frosty morning?

No, Mother, I won't get up …

What if I give you some bacon and egg,
Bacon and egg, bacon and egg …

No, Mother, I won't get up …

What if I give you a crack on the head,
Crack on the head, crack on the head …

Yes, Mother, I will get up,
Will get up, will get up.
Yes, Mother, I will get up
This cold and frosty morning.

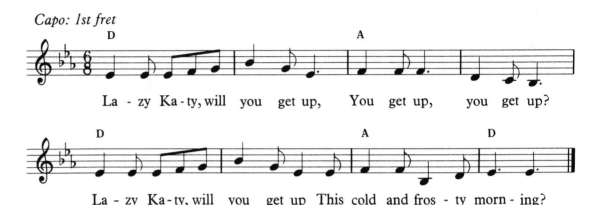

*Capo: 1st fret*

La - zy Ka - ty, will you get up, You get up, you get up?

La - zy Ka - ty, will you get up This cold and fros - ty morn - ing?

The circling ring represents the mother,
who questions her child (say the name of the
child) lying in the centre of the ring.

When the lazy (———) eventually says, 'Yes,
Mother, I will get up', she goes and chooses
a new child to be tired and sleepy.

Children enjoy making up their own
tempting bribes when trying to persuade
the lazy child to get up.

# 47 Pee, Pee, Pollyanna

*Capo: 1st fret*

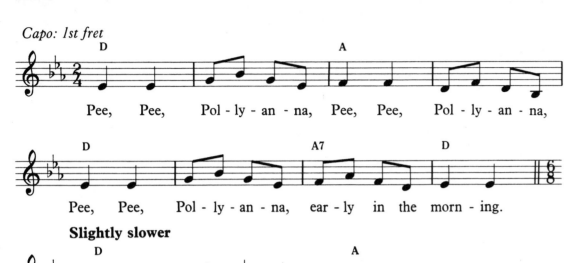

Pee, Pee, Pol-ly-an-na, Pee, Pee, Pol-ly-an-na,

Pee, Pee, Pol-ly-an-na, ear-ly in the morn-ing.

**Slightly slower**

This is the way the tea-cher stands, Folds her arms, claps her hands.

This is the way the Scots-men dance, Whoops! don't be chee – ky!

Pee, Pee, Pollyanna, Pee, Pee, Pollyanna,
Pee, Pee, Pollyanna, early in the morning.

This is the way the teacher stands.
Folds her arms, claps her hands.
This is the way the Scotsmen dance,
    Whoops! don't be cheeky!

One child skips around inside the moving circle.

On 'This is the way the teacher stands' the children stand still and do the following actions while the child in the middle also does the actions in front of a partner in the ring: on 'folds her arms' – fold arms; on 'claps her hands' – clap hands; on 'this is the way the Scotsmen dance' – attempt Highland fling; on 'Whoops! don't be cheeky' – turn outwards and flick up imaginary kilts.

The game starts again and progresses as follows: the original child and partner skip around inside the moving circle. They each choose a new partner and bring them into the circle and the game continues in this way until the circle is dissolved.

# 48 Poor Jenny sits a-weeping

Poor Jenny sits a-weeping, a-weeping, a-weeping,
Poor Jenny sits a-weeping on a bright summer's
    day.

Oh Jenny, what you weeping for, what you weeping
    for, what you weeping for,
Oh Jenny what you weeping for on a bright
    summer's day?

I'm weeping for a sweetheart, a sweetheart, a
    sweetheart,
I'm weeping for a sweetheart on a bright summer's
    day.

Stand up and choose your lover, your lover, your
    lover,
Stand up and choose your lover on a bright
    summer's day.

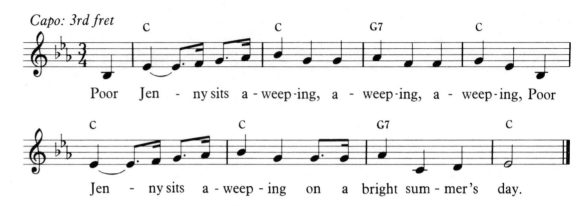

The children dance around in a circle while
'poor Jenny' sits with hands over her face
'weeping'.

'Jenny' answers the circle with the third
verse, and then stands up and chooses a new
child to be 'poor Jenny'.

# 49 The farmer's in his den

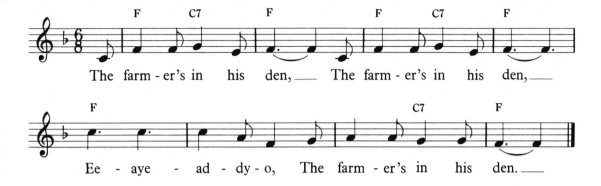

The farm-er's in his den,＿ The farm-er's in his den,＿

Ee - aye - ad - dy-o, The farm-er's in his den.＿

The farmer's in his den,
The farmer's in his den,
Ee-aye-addy-o,
The farmer's in his den.

The farmer wants a wife,
The farmer wants a wife,
Ee-aye-addy-o,
The farmer wants a wife.

The wife wants a child …

The child wants a nurse …

The nurse wants a dog …

We all pat the dog …

A boy stands in the middle of a ring of children who move around him singing.

The ring stops and the 'farmer' chooses a wife who joins him in the centre.

The wife chooses a child and the three form a small ring in the centre.

This sequence is repeated with each new character until in the last verse all the children pat the 'dog'. The dog becomes the new 'farmer'.

An alternative ending is for the dog to choose a 'bone' and then 'the bone stands alone'.

# 50 Here comes Mrs Macaroni

Here comes Mrs Macaroni,
Riding on her milk white pony,
Here she comes with all her money,
  Mrs Macaroni.

Hong-Kong, Hong-Kong, Suzyanna,
Hong-Kong, Hong-Kong, Suzyanna,
Hong-Kong, Hong-Kong, Suzyanna,
  Mrs Macaroni.

*Capo: 1st fret*

Here comes Miss-is Ma - ca - ro - ni, Ri - ding on her milk white po - ny,

Here she comes with all her mo - ney, Miss - is Ma - ca - ro - ni.

*clapping*    *etc.*

Hong-Kong, Hong-Kong, Su - zy - an - na, Hong-Kong, Hong-Kong, Su - zy - an - na,

Hong-Kong, Hong-Kong, Su - zy - an - na, Miss - is Ma - ca - ro - ni.

This game moves at a brisk pace, with a
circle of children skipping around a child in
the middle who also skips and chooses a
partner on 'Mrs Macaroni'.

At 'Hong-Kong, Hong-Kong, Suzyanna'
the children stand still and clap their hands
while the couple skip around inside the
circle, holding crossed hands.

The game starts again with the first child
returning to the circle.

# 51 Good morning, my friend

Capo: 3rd fret

Tra - la - la - la - la - la, Tra - la - la - la - la - la, Tra -
- la - la - la - la, Tra - la - la - la - la - la. Good
morn - ing, my friend, How are you to - day? Will
you come and play? That - 'll be o - kay.

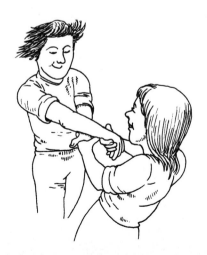

Tra-la-la-la-la-la,
Tra-la-la-la-la-la,
Tra-la-la-la-la,
Tra-la-la-la-la-la.

Good morning, my friend,
How are you today?
Will you come and play?
That'll be okay.

Tra-la-la-la-la-la,
Tra-la-la-la-la-la,
Tra-la-la-la-la,
Tra-la-la-la-la-la.

On the first chorus of 'Tra-la-la-la-la-la',
the circle of children move around one
child in the centre who skips around as well.

On 'Good morning, my friend', the child
goes and stands opposite another child in
the circle, and wags finger at her; the other
child wags back.

During the second chorus the two children
skip in the middle with hands crossed in
front of them, while the circling children
also skip around.

Then the two children separate and choose
a new partner when the verse is sung again.
This continues until the circle is no more,
and if one child is left he starts the game
again.

# 52 The big ship sails on the alley-alley-o

The big ship sails on the alley-alley-o,
  the alley-alley-o, the alley-alley-o.
Oh! the big ship sails on the alley-alley-o
  on the last day of September.

The captain says it will never, never do,
  never, never do, never, never do.
The captain says it will never, never do
  on the last day of September.

The big ship sank to the bottom of the sea,
  the bottom of the sea, the bottom of the sea.
The big ship sank to the bottom of the sea
  on the last day of September.

(Twenty-four) dollies in the washing tub,
  the washing tub, the washing tub.
(Twenty-four) dollies in the washing tub,
  *Whoops! Bang! Whee!

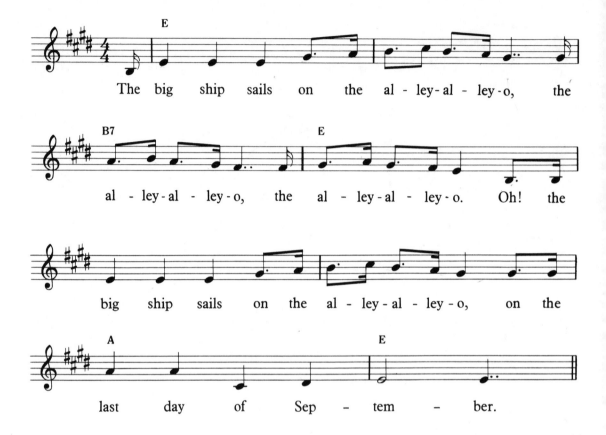

* On 'Whoops! Bang! Whee!' everyone
shakes hands in time to the song, releasing
them and jumping high on 'Whee!'

(Twen - ty four) dol - lies in the wash - ing tub, the

**B7**     **E**

wash - ing tub, the wash - ing tub.     (Twen - ty four) dol - lies in     the

**B7**

wash - ing tub,     Whoops!     Bang!     Whee!

The tallest child is chosen and the rest of the children line up and join hands. The chosen child rests his right hand against a tree or wall, making an archway, and during the first three verses the last child of the line leads the others under the archway. The tallest child finds himself being turned around but must keep his hand on the tree; his arms are now crossed in front of him, and the new archway for the line of children to go under is the tallest child's left arm and the right arm of the next child. This progression continues all the way down the line while the verses are sung.

When the last child has been 'turned', he joins hands with the first child's remaining hand, making a circle facing inwards.

Count how many children are in the circle and tug alternate hands while singing the fourth verse.

# 53 Oh! We are two sailors

Oh! We are two sailors lately come from sea,
And if you want another one, come along with me.
    Wishy-washy, wishy-washy,
    Wishy-washy-wee,
And if you want another one, come along with me.

Oh! We are two sai - lors late - ly come from sea, And

if you want an-oth - er one, come a-long with me.

Wish - y-wash - y, wish - y-wash - y, Wish - y-wash - y-wee, And

if you want an-oth - er one, come a-long with me.

The children circle around in a ring while two children dance inside with right hands joined.

On the fourth line, the two children turn and each faces someone in the ring. They place their hands on the new partner's shoulders and both swing in rhythm from one foot to another, keeping their legs straight and kicking sideways.

The two new chosen children now come to the centre of the ring and begin the game again.

# 54 Paddy from home

Pad-dy from home has ne - ver been, A rail-way train he's ne - ver seen. He

wants to go on the big mach-ine, And ride up-on the rail - way.

Paddy from home has never been,
A railway train he's never seen.
He wants to go on the big machine,
And ride upon the railway.

One child stands in the middle as 'Paddy',
while everyone else sits in a circle holding a
piece of string which has been tied at the
end to make it as big as the circle. A ring is
strung on the string which the players pass
backwards and forwards, hiding it with
their hands. 'Paddy' has to guess who has it
and when he does, the child holding the
ring is the next 'Paddy'.

# 55 Old Roger is dead

Old Roger is dead and he lies in his grave,
  Lies in his grave, lies in his grave.
Old Roger is dead and he lies in his grave,
  Ee-aye! lies in his grave.

There grew an old apple tree over his head,
  Over his head, over his head.
There grew an old apple tree over his head,
  Ee-aye! over his head.

The apples were ripe and they all fell off,
  All fell off, all fell off.
The apples were ripe and they all fell off,
  Ee-aye! all fell off.

There came an old woman a-pickin' them up,
  Pickin' them up, pickin' them up.
There came an old woman a-pickin' them up,
  Ee-aye! pickin' them up.

Old Roger got up and he gave her a knock,
  Gave her a knock, gave her a knock.
Old Roger got up and he gave her a knock
  Ee-aye! gave her a knock.

Which made the old woman go hickety-hock,
  Hickety-hock, hickety-hock.
Which made the old woman go hickety-hock,
  Ee-aye! hickety-hock.

'Old Roger' lies on his back, eyes closed,
hands clasped over his chest. A child stands
over him, hands raised like the boughs of a
tree. An 'old woman' hovers outside the
ring of children, who are moving round
'Old Roger'.

On the second verse the children stop and
hold hands over their heads like the swaying
boughs of a tree.

Then the children shake their hands and
arms and stoop to the ground, acting as if
apples had fallen to the ground, in time to
the music.

The 'old woman' comes into the ring on the
fourth verse, pretending to pick apples off
the ground and put them into her basket;
the children do the same.

'Old Roger' rises on the fifth verse and gives
the 'old woman' a shove around the ring,
and the children act likewise.

On the last verse everybody pretends to be
old and hobbled, moving around the ring.

The three characters choose three new
children and the game starts again.

# 56 Oats and beans and barley grow

Oats and beans and barley grow,
Oats and beans and barley grow.
You nor I and nobody knows
    Where oats and beans and barley grow.

First the farmer sows his seed,
Then he stands and takes his ease.
He stamps his foot, he claps his hand
    And turns around to view the land.

Do you want a partner?
Do you want a partner?
For if you do, you must be true,
    And choose one very shortly.

Now you're married you must obey,
You must be true to all you say.
You must be kind, you must be good
    And help your wife to chop the wood.

Chop it well and bring it in,
And kiss the girl who's in the ring.
Chop it well and bring it in,
    And kiss the girl who's in the ring.

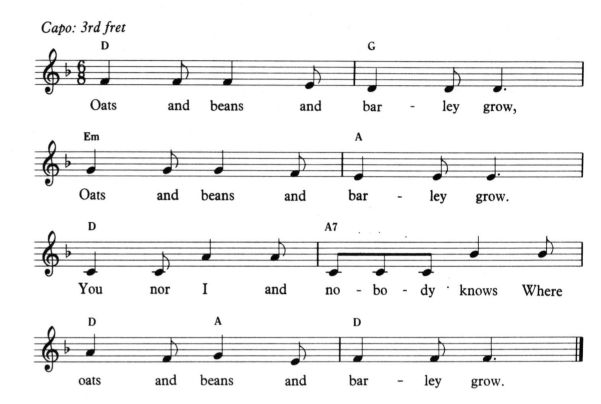

*Capo: 3rd fret*

The children skip around in a ring with a boy as the farmer in the centre.

On the second verse, they all stand still and do the following mime: pretend to scatter seed from basket in left arm; stand with feet apart and hands on hips; stamp feet and clap hands, then turn around shading eyes with hands.

On the third verse the children skip around while the farmer chooses a partner, bringing her into the ring.

On the fourth verse he leads her around the ring while the other children stand still and wag fingers at the couple.

The children clap hands during the last verse while the boy kisses the girl, leaving her to start the game over again.

# 57 I'm Shirley Temple

*This is specifically a girls' game …*

I'm Shirley Temple, the girl with curly hair,
I've got two dimples, I wear my clothes up there.
I'm not able to do the Betty Grable,
I'm Shirley Temple, the girl with curly hair.
    Oh — Salome, Salome, I can do Salome,
    Hands up there, skirts up there,
    I can do Salome.

With one girl in the centre, the children circle around, stopping and clapping hands on 'Oh Salome, Salome' through to the end.

The girl in the centre does the following: on first and third lines she puts her left hand on hip and right hand on head, wiggles her head and draws imaginary circles at the side of her head; on the second line she points to two dimples on cheeks and hoists imaginary skirt to knees. On 'Oh' she twirls around with outstretched arm pointing at a girl of her choice in the circle, and they dance around holding right hands and fling their left arms up on 'Hands up there', then hoist skirts up to knees on next line.

The chosen girl now becomes the girl for the centre and the game starts off again.

I'm Shir - ley Tem - ple, the girl with cur - ly hair, ___ I've
got two ___ dim - ples, I wear my clothes up there. I'm not
a - ble to do the Bet - ty Gra - ble, ___ I'm Shir - ley
Tem - ple, the girl with cur - ly hair. Oh — Sa -
- lo - me, ___ Sa - lo - me, I can do Sa - lo - me,
Hands up there, skirts up there, I can do Sa - lo - me.

# 58 King of the Barbarees

*... and the boys enjoy this one.*

The 'gates of the Barbarees' are two children who hold hands with arms outstretched. The 'King' and six or seven 'messengers' stand opposite.

One 'messenger' dances around the 'gates of the Barbarees' saying:

> O will you surrender, O will you surrender
> The gates of the Barbarees?

to which the 'gates' reply, shaking their arms in time to the answer:

> We won't surrender, we won't surrender
> The gates of the Barbarees.

Still dancing around, the messenger says:

> I'll tell the King, I'll tell the King,
> The King of the Barbarees.

He now goes to the King and, kneeling on one knee and raising the right hand, says:

> O King, O King, a message I bring,
> A message I bring to thee.
> They won't surrender,
> They won't surrender
> The gates of the Barbarees.

The King replies, pointing to the line of children:

> Send my second messenger.

The second messenger now joins the first child and they repeat the whole dialogue and action as before.

The King sends the third, fourth, fifth and sixth messengers until, finally, he says:

> I'll come.

At this, he takes a running jump and flings his body on to the arms of the gate, trying to break their hold. Each child follows suit until the arms of the 'gates' have broken their hold. The child who breaks the hold becomes the new King.

# 59 Round and round the village

Round and round the village,
    round and round the village,
Round and round the village,
    as we have done before.

In and out the windows,
    in and out the windows,
In and out the windows,
    as we have done before.

Stand and face your lover,
    stand and face your lover,
Stand and face your lover,
    as we have done before.

Follow her to London,
    follow her to London,
Follow her to London,
    as we have done before.

Shake hands before you leave her,
    shake hands before you leave her,
Shake hands before you leave her,
    as we have done before.

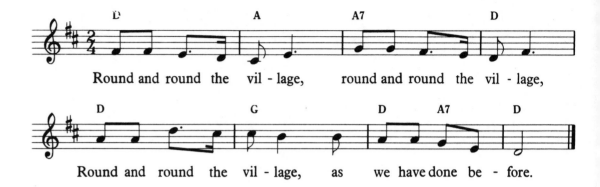

Round and round the vil - lage, round and round the vil - lage,

Round and round the vil - lage, as we have done be - fore.

The children go round in a ring while one child skips round the outside.

On the second verse they stop and raise their arms while the single child goes in and out under the arms.

She faces a partner on the third verse and then leads him under the arches, weaving in and out of the circle.

They shake hands and the first child now joins the ring for the game to begin again.

# 60  Fair Rosa

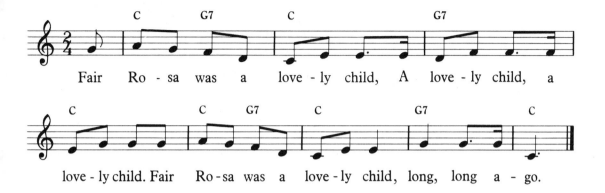

Fair Ro-sa was a love-ly child, A love-ly child, a love-ly child. Fair Ro-sa was a love-ly child, long, long a-go.

The children circle around 'Fair Rosa' who stands in the middle. The 'handsome prince' stands outside the ring and the 'wicked fairy' is inside.

On the second verse the children stand still and raise their arms, still holding hands, to make tower formation.

Then the wicked fairy moves around Fair Rosa, waving her arms and casting an imaginary spell. The ring of children do the same.

On the fourth verse Fair Rosa falls down and pretends to sleep, while the ring moves in closer to the sleeping girl, the children making their arms form branches by raising them over Fair Rosa.

The handsome prince gallops around the ring on an imaginary horse, then he goes around cutting away the branches.

The ring falls back from the sleeping princess and the prince wakes her up by kissing her hand.

These two now join hands and twirl around while the other children clap hands.

The three characters now choose three new children to play the game again.

Fair Rosa was a lovely child,
A lovely child, a lovely child.
Fair Rosa was a lovely child, long, long ago.

And she lived in a big high tower,
A big high tower, a big high tower.
And she lived in a big high tower, long, long ago.

A wicked fairy cast a spell,
Cast a spell, cast a spell.
A wicked fairy cast a spell, long, long ago.

Fair Rosa slept for a hundred years,
A hundred years, a hundred years.
Fair Rosa slept for a hundred years, long, long ago.

A great big forest grew around,
Grew around, grew around.
A great big forest grew around, long, long ago.

A handsome prince came riding by,
Riding by, riding by.
A handsome prince came riding by, long, long ago.

He took his sword and he cut it down,
Cut it down, cut it down.
He took his sword and he cut it down, long, long ago.

He kissed Fair Rosa's lily white hand,
Lily white hand, lily white hand.
He kissed Fair Rosa's lily white hand, long, long ago.

And everybody's happy now,
Happy now, happy now.
And everybody's happy now, long, long ago.

# 61 In and out the rushing bluebells

In and out the rushing bluebells,
In and out the rushing bluebells,
In and out the rushing bluebells,
    You are my master.

Tippa-rippa-rappa on my shoulder,
Tippa-rippa-rappa on my shoulder,
Tippa-rippa-rappa on my shoulder,
    You are my master.

The children stand in a ring holding hands with arms raised, while one child weaves in and out of the archways.

The child stops behind someone and pats on his shoulder in time to the music. This chosen child now leads off with the original child hanging on to the 'tail' of the new leader. They weave in and out of the arches before stopping behind a new 'leader'.

The game carries on until only two children are left forming the archway. This is a good opportunity to go into a new game of 'London Bridge is falling down'.

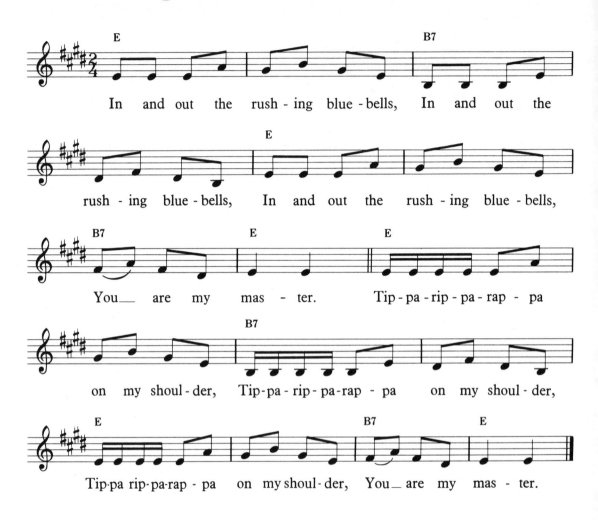

# 62 London Bridge is falling down

Lon - don Bridge is fall - ing down, Fall - ing down, fall - ing down.

Lon - don Bridge is fall - ing down, My fair la - dy. —

This is an interesting variant to the usually-known version.

Two children hold hands to make an arch, and agree between themselves the objects they will represent, for example gold or silver, rose or lily, etc. The rest of the children skip under the arch until one of them is caught at the end of the first verse and has to choose which side to go to. Depending on how many children there are, the 'arch' decides how many times to sing each verse.

On the second verse the children forming the arch bend their knees, lowering the height of the bridge and catch another child on 'My fair lady'.

On the last verse they squat on their haunches, making the bridge even lower.

The prisoners stand behind the leaders until all are caught and the game ends with a tug-of-war. (The dividing line for the tug-of-war can be chalked, or a hanky or piece of string laid on the ground.)

London Bridge is falling down,
    Falling down, falling down.
London Bridge is falling down,
    My fair lady.

London Bridge is halfway down,
    Halfway down, halfway down.
London Bridge is halfway down,
    My fair lady.

London Bridge is all fall down,
    All fall down, all fall down.
London Bridge is all fall down,
    My fair lady.

# Folk Songs

This isn't a representative selection of the variety of British folk songs. A far bigger collection would be needed with a scholarly account of the origins and historical backgrounds to do them justice. Rather it is a collection of songs that people vividly remember singing when they were children. Many were learnt at an impressionable age from their own friends, or through close contact with an adult. When singing 'Old daddy fox' for me, Mr Mawson described how his father would sing these songs, with his grandchildren around him in the kitchen, and they would 'lap them up like milk in the morning', while Mrs Freda Palmer at the age of thirteen sat daily making gloves with her aunt who sang as they worked. In using these songs I have found an immediate response from children of today, proving that although times change, through songs that tell a story or make you laugh or cry, the wonder of childhood remains the same. However, I think it should be realised that these years of innocence are becoming fewer. Through commercialism aimed at a young adult audience the mass media are conditioning the musical tastes of youngsters at increasingly earlier years.

   Although the songs were originally learnt from a variety of people, they have been naturally adapted through use by me and are written down as such. You are about to go through the same process as you learn them in order to share with your children, and I hope the following suggestions will be of help in learning and teaching a song:

1   It is essential to know the song by heart before you plan to teach it. One way of doing this is to prepare a cassette tape of yourself singing the song or group of songs you are planning to teach. At any odd moment play this back to yourself, and in this way you will unconsciously assimilate the material over a period of time.
2   As soon as possible, memorize odd phrases that appeal to you because of their language or humour. Gradually build these phrases up, looking out for them as you listen and relisten. Sing along with the tape.

3　You are now at the stage of consciously singing through the song, using the printed page as a prompter only. Here are some guidelines:
(a) focus your attention on the story line
(b) visualize the events
(c) remember the phrases that appealed to you originally.

4　When you feel confident about the song, present it to the children. It is very important to make sure that the pitch is comfortable for them; for a long time, there has been a tendency to force children to sing up, out of their normal range. C to D is the highest you should ever go, and middle C to B the lowest.

5　The tunes are appealing and evoke certain moods, but the words tell the story and make the sense of the song, so never hurry your words; try to sing them as you would speak them. Remember you are the vehicle for the song and are planting impressions on the mind's eye and the listening ear.

Here is an example of how to teach 'Three men they went a-hunting' (No. 74):

When introducing the song, try and focus the child's attention on to a particular point that will arise or that he can relate to, e.g:

'There are these three men, an Englishman, a Scotsman and Pat – who's Pat? They go out hunting, and the first field they come to they see a haystack. The Englishman says, "It's a haystack", the Scotsman, because he's a bit miserable, says "Nay" – let me hear you say "Nay" … and Pat, because he's shortsighted and got a vivid imagination thinks it's something else. I wonder what?

'The next field they come to they find a hedgehog. The Englishman says, "It's a hedgehog." What do you think the Scotsman says? … Yes, "Nay" – and Pat thinks it's something else again.'…

Treat all the verses in the same way, getting the children used to the phrases and involved in saying them. By this time they should have said 'Nay' three times, and before even having heard the song they are familiar with the characters and story line. Ask them to say 'Nay' when you sing the first verse.

At the end of the chorus, stop and get them to sing the last line of the chorus, after you have sung it again for them to hear. Then, at the end of the third verse, stop and teach the whole chorus line by line.

Usually by this stage the children are joining in as the repetitive words and melody become implanted in their minds. At the end of the song, repeat what Pat thought the haystack, hedgehog, ship at sea and cow-clap were, and then sing the song through once more.

Build up a repertoire of songs with a wide variety of moods and use them as they have been used for generations – as an experience to share in humour, sadness and sheer enjoyment of singing.

# 63 The funny family

Once long ago, there lived a funny man,
His name was Icka-rocka-icka-rocka-ran.
His legs were long and his feet were small,
    And he couldn't walk at all.

*Chorus:*
    Eeny meeny ming mong, ping pong chow,
    Easy veasy vacka-leasy, easy veasy vow.
    Eeny meeny macka-racka, ray-ri chicka-racka
    Dominacka, lollipoppa, om pom push.

He had a wife, did this funny man,
Her name was Iddy-tiddy-ran-tan-tan.
Her legs were long, and her feet were small,
    And she couldn't walk at all.

*Chorus:*

They had children, one and two,
Chickity-cha and Chickity-choo.
Their legs were long and their feet were small,
    And they couldn't walk at all.

*Chorus:*

# 64  I have a bonnet trimmed with blue

I have a bonnet trimmed with blue.
Do you wear it? Yes, I do.
When I go to meet my John,
Then I put my bonnet on.
  Bonnet on, bonnet on,
  Then I put my bonnet on.

I have a kirtle* trimmed with green,
The prettiest one that's ever seen.
And I wear it when I can,
Going to the fair with my young man.
  My young man, my young man,
  Going to the fair with my young man.

I have a mantle trimmed with brown,
The bonniest one that's in the town.
And I wear it when I can,
Going to the fair with my young man.
  My young man, my young man,
  Going to the fair with my young man.

My young man has gone to sea,
When he comes back, he'll marry me.
He buys biscuits, I buy tarts,
Don't you think we're jolly sweethearts.
  Jolly sweethearts, jolly sweethearts,
  Don't you think we're jolly sweethearts.

*kirtle – outer petticoat or skirt

# 65 Bobby Shaftoe

Chorus Capo: 3rd fret

Bob-by Shaf-toe's gone to sea,— Sil-ver buck-les on his knee;

He'll come back and mar-ry me,— Bon-ny Bob-by Shaf-toe!

Verse

Bob-by Shaf-toe's bright and fair, Comb-ing down his yel-low hair;

He's my ain for ev-er mair, Bon-ny Bob-by Shaf-toe!

*Chorus:*
Bobby Shaftoe's gone to sea,
Silver buckles on his knee;
He'll come back and marry me,
Bonny Bobby Shaftoe!

Bobby Shaftoe's bright and fair,
Combing down his yellow hair;
He's my ain for ever mair,
Bonny Bobby Shaftoe!

*Chorus:*

Bobby Shaftoe's tall and slim,
He's always dressed so neat and trim;
The lasses they all keek at him,
Bonny Bobby Shaftoe!

*Chorus:*

Bobby Shaftoe's gett'n a bairn,
For to dangle on his airm;
In his airm and on his knee,
Bonny Bobby Shaftoe!

*Last Chorus:*
Bobby Shaftoe's been to sea,
Silver buckles on his knee;
He's come back and married me,
Bonny Bobby Shaftoe!

*ain* – own
*airm* – arm
*evermair* – evermore
*keek* – glance

# 66 The little herring

One singer or a group takes the lead in the verses and chorus.

As I was a-walking in Whitby* one day,
I spied a fishing boat out on the bay.
They caught big fish and little fish and they all
    fitted in,
And I caught for myself a fine little herring.

*Chorus:*

Oh! go on you lie.
    (*singer*) Just as I say, me lads.
Why didn't you tell me so?
    (*singer*) So I done long ago.
Well done, well done.
Don't you think I done well with my little herring?

Now what do you think that I made with his skin?
Why, a nice little house that was ever laid in.
There were big rooms and little rooms and they all
    fitted in.
Don't you think I done well with my little herring?

*Chorus:*

And what do you think that I made with his tail?
Why, a nice little ship that did ever set sail.
There were big sails and little sails and they all fitted
    in.
Don't you think I done well with my little herring?

*Chorus:*

* Sing the name of your favourite seaside
place.

And what do you think that I made with his eyes?
Why, forty plum puddings and fifty mince pies.
There were big pies and little pies and they all fitted in.
Don't you think I done well with my little herring?

*Chorus:*

And what do you think that I made with his fins?
The finest of brooches and sharpest of pins.
There were big pins and little pins and they all
    fitted in.
Don't you think I done well with my little herring?

*Chorus:*

And what do you think that I made with his bones?
Why, a nice little church that was e'er built of stones.
There were big pews and little pews and they all
    fitted in.
Don't you think I done well with my little herring?

*Chorus:*

And what do you think I made with his scales?
Hundreds of staples and thousands of nails.
There were big nails and little nails and they all
    fitted in.
Don't you think I done well with my little herring?

*Chorus:*

And what do you think that I made with his gills?
Bottles of potions and boxes of pills.
There were big pills and little pills and they all fitted in.
Don't you think I done well with my little herring?

*Chorus:*

# 67 As I was a-going down one of our streets

*Here's another song to the same tune, but with a different chorus.*

As I was a-going down one of our streets,
I met a poor boy with no shoes on his feet.
I'd plenty of money but little to spare,
So I took him to a fruit shop and bought him a
   pear.

*Chorus:*
   Toodleloo, toodlelay,
   The chorus is grand, I could sing it all day.
   Toodleloo, toodlelay,
   God bless the poor working man.

Two lovely black eyes had poor old Uncle Jim,
The boys had been throwing tomatoes at him.
Tomatoes don't hurt you, I said with a grin.
O yes they do, when they're stuffed in a tin.

*Chorus:*

I once met two beggars all tattered and torn,
They were eating the grass off of our front lawn,
I said, If you're hungry, just step round the back,
The grass is much longer and thicker than that.

*Chorus:*

I once took a note to poor old Mrs Brown,
She was having a bath and she couldn't come
   down.
I said, Oh! by golly, just slip on a tick,
But she slipped on the soap, and then she came
   quick.

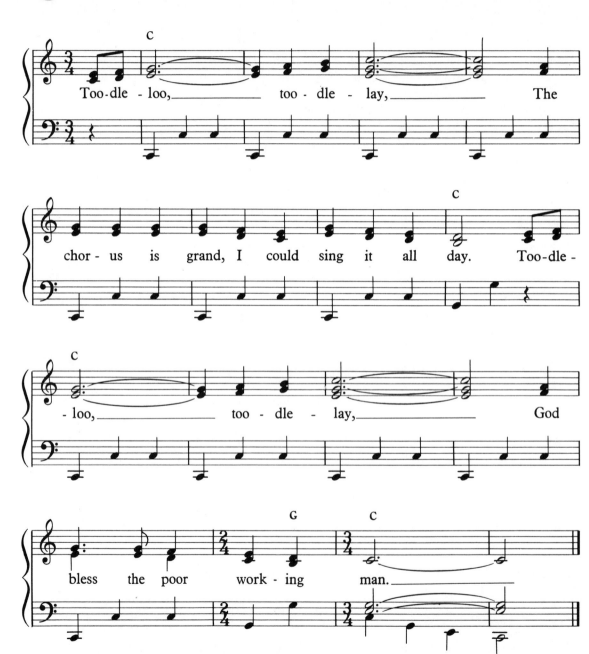

*Chorus:*

I once bought a hen in town yesterday,
And thought on the morrow an egg it would lay.
But when I awoke, Oh! I had such a shock,
The hen said, You can't have an egg, I'm a cock!

*Chorus:*

I dreamt I did die and to heaven did go.
Where do you come from? they wanted to know.
I said, I'm from Witney. St Peter did stare,
He said, Step in quick, you're the first one from
there.

*Chorus:*

# 68    Whose pigs are these?

Whose pigs are these? Whose pigs are these? They
are John Cook's, I know by the looks, And they
live in the vic - ar - age gar - den.

*Try singing this as a round.*

Whose pigs are these?
Whose pigs are these?
They are John Cook's, I know by their looks,
And they live in the vicarage garden.

# 69 When I was a lad on me father's farm

When I was a lad on me father's farm
  In the merry, merry month of May.
I used to feed the ducks and hens
  In the merry, merry month of May.
They were (*quacking*\*) here, and (*clucking*) there,
And (*clucking*) here, and (*quacking*) there,
  In the merry, merry month of May.

When I was a lad on me father's farm
  In the merry, merry, month of May.
I used to feed the cow and calves
  In the merry, merry month of May.
They were (*mooing*) here, and (*mooing*) there,
And (*mooing*) here, and (*mooing*) there,
  In the merry, merry month of May.

When I was a lad on me father's farm
  In the merry, merry month of May.
I used to feed the sheep and lambs
  In the merry, merry month of May.
They were (*maa-ing*) here, and (*baa-ing*) there,
And (*baa-ing*) here, and (*maa-ing*) there,
  In the merry, merry month of May.

\* Make suitable animal noises.

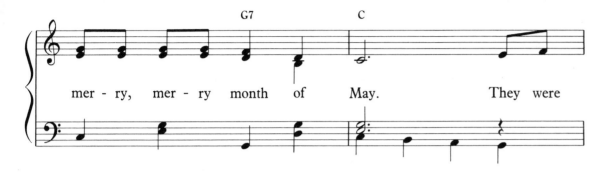

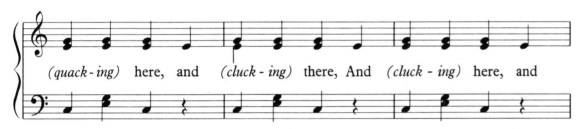

When I was a lad on me father's farm
  In the merry, merry month of May.
I used to feed his two donkeys
  In the merry, merry month of May.
They were (*braying*) here, and (*braying*) there,
And (*braying*) here, and (*braying*) there,
  In the merry, merry month of May.

When I was a lad on me father's farm
  In the merry, merry month of May.
I used to feed the sow and pigs
  In the merry, merry month of May.
They were (*snorting*) here, and (*snorting*) there,
And (*snorting*) here, and (*snorting*) there,
  In the merry, merry month of May.

# 70  Me grandfather died

Me grandfather died and he left me a mule,
A silly old mule, and he followed me to school.

*Chorus:*
And it's ee-aye-addy-o,
Mammy and your daddy-o,
Ee-aye-addy-o,
Down by the Lucan* dairy.

Me grandfather died and he left me a pig,
A fat little pig and he danced me a jig.

*Chorus:*

Me grandfather died and he left me a hen,
A fat little hen and she laid now and then.

*Chorus:*

Me grandfather died and he left me an ass,
A stupid old ass and he followed me to mass.

*Chorus:*

Me grandfather died and he left me a drake,
A fat little drake, he was swallowed by a snake.

*Chorus:*

* Lucan dairy is in an area in Dublin.

# 71 Johnny Baloo

Let's go in the woods, said Robin to Bobbin,
Let's go in the woods, said Richard to Robin,
Let's go in the woods, said Johnny Baloo,
Let's go in the woods, lads, every one.

What will we do there? said Robin to Bobbin,
What will we do there? said Richard to Robin,
What will we do there? said Johnny Baloo,
What will we do there, lads, every one?

We'll catch a green rabbit, said Robin to Bobbin,
We'll catch a green rabbit, said Richard to Robin,
We'll catch a green rabbit, said Johnny Baloo,
We'll catch a green rabbit, lads, every one.

What will we do with it? said Robin to Bobbin,
What will we do with it? said Richard to Robin,
What will we do with it? said Johnny Baloo,
What will we do with it, lads, every one?

We'll give it to the Queen, said Robin to Bobbin,
We'll give it to the Queen, said Richard to Robin,
We'll give it to the Queen, said Johnny Baloo,
We'll give it to the Queen, lads, every one.

Will she be pleased? said Robin to Bobbin,
Will she be pleased? said Richard to Robin,
Of course she'll be pleased, said Johnny Baloo,
She'll give us a knighthood, every one.

# 72 Old daddy fox

The fox went out one winter's night,
Called to the moon to give him light.
Long way to go, over the snow,
Before he got to his den-o!
    Den-o! Den-o!
Long way to go, over the snow,
Before he got to his den-o!

At last he came to the farmer's yard,
Where the ducks and the geese were cackling hard.
That their nerves should be shaken and their rest so
    marred
By a visit from old daddy fox-o!
    Fox-o! Fox-o!
That their nerves should be shaken and their rest so
    marred
By a visit from old daddy fox-o!

He seized the grey goose by the neck,
Threw him over across his back,
The grey goose cried out, Quack! Quack! Quack!
But the fox was off to his den-o!
    Den-o! Den-o!
The grey goose cried out …

Old Mrs Slipper Slopper jumped out of bed,
Out of the window she popped her head:
John, John, John, the grey goose is gone
And the fox is off to his den-o!
    Den-o! Den-o!
John, John, John …

John ran up to the top of the hill,
Blew his horn both loud and shrill.
Oh! said the fox, That's better music still,
But I'd rather be here in me den-o!
    Den-o! Den-o!
Oh! said the fox …

Old daddy fox went back to his den,
And his dear little foxes eight, nine, ten.
Daddy, you must go there again,
For sure 'tis a lucky town-o!
    Town-o! Town-o!
Daddy you must go …

Old Daddy fox and his good wife
Carved up the goose without fork or knife,
Said 'twas the best they'd tasted in their life,
And the little ones chewed on the bones-o!
    Bones-o! Bones-o!
Said 'twas the best …

# 73 Babes in the wood

One day don't you know, and a long time ago,
These two little children whose names I don't
know,
Were stolen away, on a fine summer's day,
And lost in the wood as I've heard the folk say.
Poor babes in the wood, poor babes in the wood;
Don't you remember the babes in the wood?

And when it was night, so sad was their plight,
The sun it went down and the moon gave no
light.
They sobbed and they sighed, and they bitterly
cried,
These poor little children, they lay down and
died.
Poor babes in the wood, poor babes in the wood;
Don't you remember the babes in the wood?

And when they were dead, the robins so red
Brought strawberry leaves and over them
spread;
And all the day long in the branches among,
They mournfully whistled and this was their
song.
Poor babes in the wood, poor babes in the wood;
Don't you remember the babes in the wood?

One day don't you know, and a long time a - go, These
two lit - tle chil - dren whose names I don't know, Were
stol - en a - way, on a fine sum - mer's day, And

lost in the wood as I've heard the folk say._____

Poor babes in the wood, poor babes in the wood;

Don't you re - mem - ber the babes in the wood?

# 74 Three men they went a-hunting

Three men they went a-hunting,
And nothing could they find,
Till at last they came to a haystack,
And that they left behind.
The Englishman said it was a haystack,
The Scotsman he said nay,
But Pat said bedad it's an elephant
Wi' its trunk all blown away.

*Chorus:*
I saw her, I saw her,
I saw her at the window.
If you don't come down and let me in,
By golly, I'll smash the window.

Three men they went a-hunting,
And nothing could they find,
Till at last they came to a hedgehog,
And that they left behind.
The Englishman said it was a hedgehog,
The Scotsman he said nay,
But Pat said bedad it's a pincushion
With pins stuck in the wrong way.

*Chorus:*

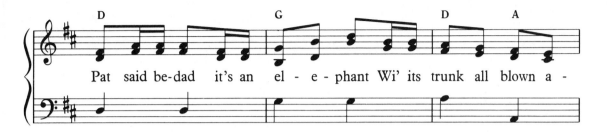

Pat said be-dad it's an el - e - phant Wi' its trunk all blown a -

-way. I saw her, I saw her, I

saw her at the win - dow. If you don't come down and

let me in, By gol - ly, I'll smash the win - dow.

Three men they went a-hunting,
And nothing could they find,
Till at last they came to a black pig,
And that they left behind.
The Englishman said it was a black pig,
The Scotsman he said nay,
But Pat said bedad it's the devil himself
And all three ran away.

*Chorus:*

Three men they went a-hunting,
And nothing could they find,
Till at last they came to a ship at sea,
And that they left behind.
The Englishman said it was a ship at sea,
The Scotsman he said nay,
But Pat said bedad it's old Ireland
Come flipping down this way.

*Chorus:*

Three men they went a-hunting,
And nothing could they find,
Till at last they came to a cow-clap,
And that they left behind.
The Englishman said it was a cow clap,
The Scotsman he said nay,
But Pat said bedad it's a custard,
Wi' its crust all blown away.

*Chorus:*

# 75  A Highland lullaby

I left my baby lying there,
Lying there, lying there,
I left my baby lying there,
To go and gather blaeberries.

*Chorus:*

*Hovan hovan gorry og o,
Gorry og o, gorry og o,
Hovan hovan gorry og o,
But never found my baby-o.

I saw the wee brown otter's track,
Otter's track, otter's track,
I saw the wee brown otter's track,
But never found my baby-o.

*Chorus:*

\* *pronounced* hoe-van go-rēach oh

I saw the swan's nest on the loch,
On the loch, on the loch,
I saw the swan's nest on the loch,
   But never found my baby-o.

*Chorus:*

I saw the track of the yellow deer,
Yellow deer, yellow deer,
I saw the track of the yellow deer,
   But never found my baby-o.

*Chorus:*

I heard the curlew crying high,
Crying high, crying high,
I heard the curlew crying high,
But never found my baby-o.

*Chorus:*

# 76 The fox and the grey goose

The fox jumped up on a moon-light night, The star-s were shin-ing and all things bright._____ A - ha! said the fox, it's a ve-ry fine night_____ For me to go through the town die - o, For me to go through the town._____

The fox jumped up on a moonlight night,
The stars were shining and all things bright.
  Aha! said the fox, it's a very fine night
  For me to go through the town die-o,
  For me to go through the town.

The fox when he came to yonder stile,
He lifted his ears and listened awhile.
  Aha! said the fox, it's but a short mile
  From this to yonder town die-o,
  From this to yonder town.

The fox when he came to the farmer's gate,
Who should he see but the farmer's drake.
  I love you well for your master's sake
  But I long to be picking your bones aye-o
  But I long to be picking your bones.

The grey goose ran around the stack,
Aha! said the fox, for you're very fat,
  You'll do very well to ride on my back
  From this to yonder town die-o,
  From this to yonder town.

The farmer's wife she jumped out of bed,
And out of the window she popped her head.
  O husband, O husband, the geese are all dead,
  The fox has been through the town die-o,
  The fox has been through the town.

The farmer he loaded his pistol with lead,
And shot the old rogue of a fox through the head,
  Aha! said the farmer, I think you're quite dead,
  No more you will trouble the town die-o,
  No more you will trouble the town.

# 77 Young folks, old folks, everybody come

*Chorus:*

Young folks, old folks, everybody come
To our little Sunday school and we'll have lots
    of fun.
Bring your toffee apples, sit down upon the
    floor,
And we'll tell you Bible stories that you've
    never heard before.

Adam was the first man, Eve was his spouse;
They got together and started keeping house:
Had one son, Abel was his name,
And everything was fine until they started raising
    Cain.

*Chorus:*

Essau was a fella with a very hairy chest,
This chest it was so hairy, he'd no need to wear a
    vest;
His father left him property not very far from
    Norwich
But the darn fool wet his socks in a bowl full of
    porridge.

*Chorus:*

Adam was a good man, children he had seven,
Thought he'd hire a donkey cart and take them all
    to heaven;
Strange to say he lost his way altho' he knew it well,
Over went the donkey cart and sent them all to hell.

*Chorus:*

*And here's a verse that's sung in America:*

David was a wise guy, a wiry little cuss,
Along came Goliath looking for a fuss;
David fetched a stone, conked him on the dome,
And Goliath heard the birdies singing 'Home Sweet
    Home'.

*Chorus and first verse*

Young folks, old folks, ev'-ry-bo-dy come\_\_

To our lit-tle Sun-day school and we'll have lots of fun.\_\_

Bring your toff-ee ap-ples,\_\_ sit down up-on the floor, And we'll

tell you Bib-le stor-ies that you've nev-er heard be-fore.\_\_

# 78 Johnny's lost his marble

Johnny's lost his marble,
Johnny's lost his marble,
Johnny's lost his marble,
Down in granny's yard.

He lost it up the drainpipe,
He lost it up the drainpipe,
He lost it up the drainpipe,
Down in granny's yard.

He went and got the clothes prop ...

He rammed it up the drainpipe ...

Still he didn't find it ...

So he went and got the terrier ...

He tied it to the clothes prop ...

And he rammed it up the drainpipe ...

Still he didn't find it ...

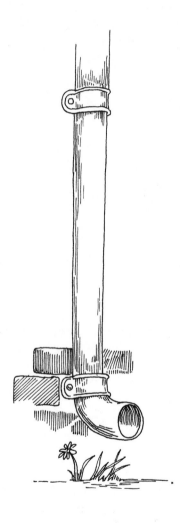

So he went and got the policeman ...

And he tied him to the clothes prop ...

He rammed him up the drainpipe ...

Still he didn't find it ...

So he went and got gunpowder ...

He tied it to the clothes prop ...

He rammed it up the drainpipe,
He rammed it up the drainpipe,
He rammed it up the drainpipe,
And BLEW UP Granny's yard.

Johnny's found his marble ...

Twas in his blooming pocket,
Twas in his blooming pocket,
Twas in his blooming pocket,
DOWN IN GRANNY'S YARD.

Johnny's lost his marble, ___ Johnny's lost his marble, ___

Johnny's lost his marble, ___ Down in granny's yard.

# 79 When I was single

*Chorus:*
Oh when I was single, me pockets did jingle,
I wish I was single again.
For when I was single, me pockets did jingle,
I wish I was single again.

I married a wife, oh then and oh then,
I married a wife, oh then.
Oh I married a wife, she's the plague of my life,
    And I wish I was single again.

*Chorus:*

My wife took the fever, oh then and oh then,
My wife took the fever, oh then,
My wife took the fever, I hope it don't leave her,
    I wish I was single again.

*Chorus:*

During the chorus do the following
clapping routine in rhythm to the song:
slap left hand on left knee, slap right hand
on right knee, clap hands together. Repeat
pattern.

My wife she died, oh then and oh then,
My wife she died, oh then.
My wife she died, I laughed 'til I cried,
And I found myself single again.

*Chorus:*

I married another, oh then and oh then,
I married another, oh then.
I married another, she's worse than the other,
I wish I was single again.

*Last chorus:*

For when I was single, me pockets did jingle,
I wish I was single again.
For when I was single, me pockets did jingle,
I wish I was single again.

# 80　There were three Jews from Jerusalem

There were three Jews from Jerusalem,
There were three Jews from Jerusalem.
  Jerry, Jerry, Jerry, slam, slam, slam,
  Jerry, Jerry, Jerry, slam, slam, slam,
There were three Jews from Jerusalem.

Now the first Jew's name was Abraham,
The first Jew's name was Abraham.
  Abra, Abra, Abra, ham, ham, ham,
  Abra, Abra, Abra, ham, ham, ham,
The first Jew's name was Abraham.

Now the second Jew's name was Isaac,
The second Jew's name was Isaac.
  Issy, Issy, Issy, zac, zac, zac,
  Issy, Issy, Issy, zac, zac, zac,
The second Jew's name was Isaac.

Now the third Jew's name was Gabriel,
The third Jew's name was Gabriel.
  Gabri, Gabri, Gabri, hal, hal, hal,
  Gabri, Gabri, Gabri, hal, hal, hal,
The third Jew's name was Gabriel.

Now they went for a ride in a charabanc,
They went for a ride in a charabanc.
  Chara, chara, chara, bang, bang, bang,
  Chara, chara, chara, bang, bang, bang,
They went for a ride in a charabanc.

They came to the edge of a precipice,
They came to the edge of a precipice.
  Pressa, pressa, pressa, wee, wee, wee,
  Pressa, pressa, pressa, wee, wee, wee,
They came to the edge of a precipice.

Now we must finish it,
Now we must finish it.
  Fini, fini, fini, la, la, la,
  Fini, fini, fini, la, la, la,
And now we must finish it.

There were three Jews from Je - ru - sa - lem, There were three Jews from Je-

-ru - sa - lem. Jer - ry, Jer - ry, Jer - ry, slam, slam, slam,

Jer - ry, Jer - ry, Jer - ry, slam, slam, slam, There were three

Jews___ from Je ru sa lem.

# Index of first lines